Battleground

VILLERS-BRE

With the continued expansion of the Battleground series a **Battleground Series Club** has been formed to benefit the reader. The purpose of the Club is to keep members informed of new titles and to offer many other reader-benefits. Membership is free and by registering an interest you can help us predict print runs and thus assist us in maintaining the quality and prices at their present levels.

Please call the office 01226 734555, or send your name and address along with a request for more information to:

Battleground Series Club Pen & Sword Books Ltd,
47 Church Street, Barnsley, South Yorkshire S70 2AS

Battleground Europe
VILLERS-BRETONNEUX

Peter Pedersen

To my Father and in loving memory of my Mother

Great War series editor
Nigel Cave

Pen & Sword
MILITARY

Cover: *13 Brigade Attack at Villers-Bretonneux* by Will Longstaff (AWM ART 03028)

Other books by Peter Pedersen:
Monash as Military Commander
Images of Gallipoli
Hamel (Battleground Europe series)
Fromelles (Battleground Europe series)

First published in Great Britain in 2004 by
Pen & Sword Military
an imprint of
Pen & Sword Books Ltd
47 Church Street
Barnsley
South Yorkshire
S70 2AS

ISBN 1 84415 061 5

For a complete list of Pen & Sword titles, please contact
Pen & Sword Books Limited
47 Church Street, Barnsley, South Yorkshire, S70 2AS, England
E-mail: enquiries@pen-and-sword.co.uk
Website: www.pen-and-sword.co.uk

CONTENTS

The remains of the red château, a remarkable relic of the war on the Western
Front, in particular the fighting around Villers-Bretonneux, after it was
destroyed to make way for a supermarket,
by permission of the local authority in August 2004.
Incredibilis superbia!

INTRODUCTION BY SERIES EDITOR

This is another fine contribution to the *Battleground Europe* series by Dr Peter Pedersen. It is a model of clarity in describing two complex battles around Villers-Bretonneux in April 1918, and has the same lucidity and even-handed judgements of his Hamel, a battle fought nearby, and Fromelles, in French Flanders.

Villers-Bretonneux is now a town much associated by the military historian with Australia; and this is reflected in the close links today's commune has with that country – in the excellent museum, in the name of a street and, of course, in the impressive memorial to the missing dead of Australia who fell in France (those in Belgium are on the Menin Gate). It was the last of the great Commonwealth Memorials to the Missing to be built, and the only one to be unveiled by George VI. The connection was also shown by the selection of an unknown Australian soldier from a cemetery on this battlefield to become the Unknown Australian Soldier in Canberra. The saving of Villers-Bretonneux, in particular during the second battle on 24-5 April, was amongst the finest achievements of the Australians. It is notable how 'modern' that battle seems – aircraft and tanks, small unit actions and the like. What might appear alien to others is the appearance of the cavalry and the important, if not crucial, part it played in the operations. Indeed the lack of cavalry was a significant factor in the failure of the Germans to take full advantage of the breakthrough that had been gained – perhaps better to say almost gained – by their other fighting arms.

Although the allied success here owed much to the Australian soldier and his commanders, the role of the British has not been downplayed; just as rightful criticism has been made as well. The British formations involved had been engaged in desperate fighting, some since the German onslaught began on 21 March, and were severely undermanned. By the time of the second German onslaught in late April, they were dependent on large numbers of new conscript recruits. Not surprisingly, their performance was often below par.

Villers-Bretonneux is a fine example of how the fighting of 1918 was so very different from that of earlier years in the war – just as the fighting of 1917 was different from 1916. It is not just the Australian pilgrim who should come to these fields, so close to the Somme valley, to pay tribute to remarkable men. What took place in them also serves to show everyone that lessons were learnt in the Great War and that skill at all levels, determination, loyalty and mutual dependence were essential elements in winning the war.

Nigel Cave Vimy Ridge 2004

AUTHOR'S INTRODUCTION

Straddling the road and railway into Amiens on the southern side of the Somme, the town of Villers-Bretonneux was a backwater until the great German *Michael* Offensive reached it at the end of March 1918. Coming close on 4 April, the Germans finally succeeded in taking it on 24 April but were ejected by the Australians in one of the war's great feats of arms. A largely Australian counterattack had also kept them at bay earlier. Saving Villers-Bretonneux meant saving Amiens, which thrust the town onto centre stage and forever associated the Australians with it.

British divisions were the defenders on both occasions and the Australians criticised their performance to the extent that the high command saw fit to intervene. But those divisions had been in action almost from the start of the German offensive and were exhausted. One of them, the 18th Division, fought at Villers-Bretonneux for longer than any other division, British or Australian, and ranked it alongside Ypres, Messines, Thiepval, and Cambrai as 'one of the place-names that spring sharply to the memory of anyone who was in the war'.[1] The British cavalry played a prominent part in stemming the German tide – as the Australians themselves acknowledged. This book fully describes the British contribution and seeks to give credit where it is due.

The fighting saw the first ever tank duel. It also encompassed a series of largely forgotten actions at nearby Hangard that achieved nothing but heavy casualties. Hangard raises the question of whether the commanders gave their men the best chance of success. The question is even more pertinent in relation to the 24 April counterattack at Villers-Bretonneux, the preparations for which were muddled to say the least.

Finally, the fog of war around the town was thick, literally and metaphorically, throughout April and the battles very fluid. Consequently, unit war diaries and personal accounts sometimes differed over the times and locations of events or were rather vague. The British Official Historian acknowledged the problem and the detailed work of the Australian Official Historian occasionally reflects it. Nonetheless, the fighting readily breaks down into battalion, company and even platoon actions that can be located on the ground and easily followed. Together, they made Villers-Bretonneux historically significant. They also made it significant as a place where mighty deeds were done.

P.A. Pedersen Sydney, Australia

ACKNOWLEDGEMENTS

This book could not have been written without the unstinting support of my father during the part of each year that I spend at my desk in Sydney. As always, Dad, I owe you more than I can say.

In France, Nicolas Goret's help was indispensable. Bombarded with queries over many months, he replied promptly with a wealth of information and also provided many of the photographs and maps. The hours I spent on the battlefields with him were as instructive as they were enjoyable, especially with regard to unravelling the mess the A29 autoroute has made of the local road network. Nicolas lives in Hamel and his website, *http://hamelfriends.free.fr*, is an essential tool for anyone studying the battles in the area or wishing to visit the battlefields. Claude Pecquet, head of the Association Villers Mémoire, clarified aspects of the town's history and contributed photographs as well. Jean-Pierre Thierry, President of the France-Australia Association in Villers-Bretonneux, gave me the run of the ANZAC Museum. As usual, Anais Bertoux lent enthusiastic support!

In England, Professor Peter Simkins of the Centre for First World War Studies at the University of Birmingham generously let me have a copy of his landmark study of the battle, which covers the fighting from the British perspective. He sent a steady stream of useful material, answered questions as they arose and read the manuscript. I greatly valued his advice. John Bourne of the Centre allowed me to use his work on some of the British commanders. Richard Jeffs of the Oxfordshire and Buckinghamshire Light Infantry Museum helped clarify discrepancies in the war diaries of some British units. I would also like to record the assistance of Peter Duckers, Curator of the Shropshire Regimental Museum, Jon-Paul Carr of the Northamptonshire Regiment Museum, Roderick Suddaby, Keeper of Written Records at the Imperial War Museum, and the Reading Room staff at The National Archives in London.

In Australia, no request was too great for Ursula Davidson, Librarian at the Royal United Service Institution of New South Wales, or Ian Smith, Senior Curator of Official and Private Records at the Australian War Memorial. I would like to say thank you, too, to its Reading Room staff.

ADVICE TO TRAVELLERS

Visitors from the battlefields north of the Somme should leave the Albert ring road at the D42 exit south of the town and follow the D42 past Meaulte and through Morlancourt and Sailly-Laurette before turning right onto the N29 at Lamotte-Warfusée. Villers-Bretonneux lies dead ahead. Those approaching from Amiens should simply stay on the N29 after it exits the city.

A dud on the shoulder of the A29 autoroute.

Before leaving check that you have appropriate vehicle cover. Full personal insurance is also strongly recommended. Take an E111 Form, obtainable from your post office, for reciprocal medical and hospital cover in France and make sure your tetanus vaccination is current. A hat, waterproof smock and sun cream are essential as the Somme weather often packs the four seasons into an hour. Do not forget binoculars, because the battlefield is extensive and picking out locations is difficult without them. A compass will help you orient the maps in this book to the ground. Good hiking shoes or boots are a must. As most of the area is farmland, stay on the roads, tracks and the edges of the fields. Drivers should be careful not to obstruct agricultural vehicles. As car break-ins are increasing on the Somme, keep valuables out of sight in the boot. Leave any dud ammunition you see well alone.

Housing Australian artefacts from the Western Front, audio-visual displays and a substantial photographic collection, the ANZAC Museum in the primary school at 9 Rue Victoria, Villers-Bretonneux is well worth a visit. The opening hours are 10 am-12.30 pm and 2-6 pm Wednesday to Saturday, and 2-6 pm Tuesdays and on the first and third Sundays each month. Contact 03-22-968079 (tel/fax) or museeaustralien@aol.com.

While Amiens and Albert offer a range of accommodation, the following list of hotels, inns and bed and breakfasts may be useful for those wishing to stay locally:

Hotels/Inns

9

Hôtel de l'Abbatiale, 9 Place Jean Catelas, 80800 CORBIE
Tel: 33 322 48 40 48 (Closed Sundays)
Hôtel de la Marine, 6 Place Roger Salengro, 80800 CORBIE
Tel: 33 322 48 01 51 (Closed weekends)
Le Logis du Santerre, 2 Rue Raoul Defruit, 80131 HARBONNIERES
Tel: 33 322 85 80 17

Bed and Breakfast
Jean Marie Van Den Bosch, 42 Rue Emile Bazin, 80800 AUBIGNY
 Tel: 33 322 48 42 47
Jean BOUCHE, 1 Rue de L'Abbaye, 80720 MARCELCAVE
Tel: 33 322 42 35 91
Isabelle DESSAINT, 6 Rue de Lamotte, 80170 BAYONVILLERS
Tel: 33 322 85 85 84

Caravan and Camp Sites (April to end October)
La Source, 7 Rue du Port, 80800 SAILLY-LAURETTE
Tel: 33 686 08 57 98
Les Puits Tournants, 6 Rue du Marais, 80800 SAILLY-LE-SEC
Tel: 33 322 76 65 56

Additional information can be found at *www.somme-tourisme.com.*

Area Map

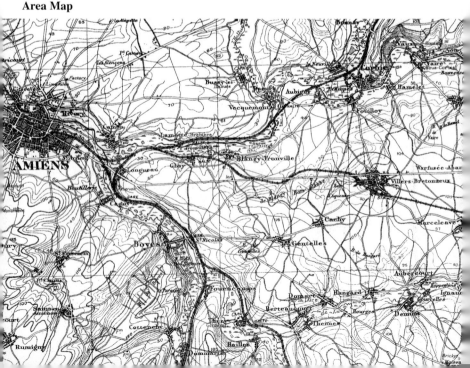

MAPS

The trench maps of the Villers-Bretonneux battlefields require some getting used to. As the area had not been fought over before, they show no clearly defined front line but just the odd squiggle here and there, reflecting the posts and trench fragments dug where each side ended up after an attack or counterattack. Sometimes the positions reported turned out to be erroneous, while the seesaw nature of the fighting meant that maps were soon out of date. On top of all this, in the 1:20,000 France series, which has the necessary topographic detail, the battlefield is spread over two maps, the divide occurring inconveniently just to the east of the town. I have used Sheet 62dSE, Edition 2A, correct as at 22 April 1918, and Sheet 62dSW, Edition 2A (Local), correct as at 9 May 1918. Both should be available from the Department of Printed Books at the Imperial War Museum in London (0171-416-5348) or the Western Front Association – if you are a member.

Locations on trench maps have been given according to the reference system used at the time. Maps were divided into squares covering an area 6,000 yards by 6,000 yards. Each was identified by a letter of the alphabet and further subdivided into six rows of six squares, making a total of 36 consecutively numbered squares each measuring 1,000 by 1,000 yards. Every one of these squares was broken down into four smaller sub-squares that were lettered

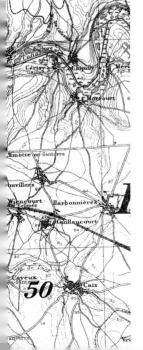

clockwise as a,b,d,c. The eastings and northings in each sub-square were then subdivided in intervals of ten and marked off thus on two sides. As an example, the railway crossed the Roman Road (the N29) at O.28.d.3.4.

Turning to modern maps, the area covered by this guide extends across four in the 1:25,000 IGN Blue Series: Sheets 2408O (Albert), 2409O (Harbonnières), 2308E (Corbie) and 2309E (Moreuil). You guessed it, Villers-Bretonneux lies at the junction of all four! At the time of writing they had not been updated to show the A29 autoroute passing to the south of the town and the resulting changes to the adjacent roads and tracks. I have included them on the tour maps but bear in mind that I am no surveyor! The IGN maps can be obtained from Waterstone's

11

Booksellers in the UK and the *Maison de la Presse* shops or major supermarkets in France. You can also order them online from IGN at *www.ign.fr*.

HOW TO USE THIS BOOK

Try to see the battlefield in your mind's eye as you read, so that you are properly prepared for the tours. Ideally, complete the drive first so that you know where the principal locations are relative to each other before you undertake the walks.

Whether you are driving or walking, there is enough detail in the battle narratives for you to focus at greater length on a particular area. Whatever you do, put the local action within the context of what was happening elsewhere, otherwise your study will lack coherence. This advice is particularly relevant to the attacks and counterattacks on 4 and 24/5 April.

Pay particular attention to the soldiers' descriptions. Their accounts of being trampled by a tank, of being in a tank that is engaging another tank and, especially, of hand-to-hand fighting in a night bayonet charge, are startlingly vivid. Breathe life into them by putting your imagination to work and you will have some idea of what Villers-Bretonneux was like at the sharp end.

1. G.H.F Nichols, *The 18th Division in the Great War* (William Blackwood, 1922), p. 302.

Chapter One

THE GERMANS APPROACH

Roman coins and villa remains are the first real clue to the otherwise obscure origins of Villers-Bretonneux, a town at the heart of northern France's Somme Department. They are evidence of the settlement that followed the arrival of Julius Caesar's legions at Amiens (or Samarobriva, as Caesar knew it), nine miles due west, in 57 BC. The earliest official reference dates from 1123, when the place was mentioned in the records of the vast Columban abbey in nearby Corbie, to whose ecclesiastical fiefdom it belonged. A village of 140 dwellings by the fourteenth century, it fed off the textile boom in Amiens in the eighteenth century and sent woven products all over Europe.

In 1914 the town boasted nine cotton mills, three brickworks and a hat factory but industrial ups-and-downs kept farming as the other mainstay. Orchards ringed much of the northern side and cereals, potatoes and sugar-beet shared the surrounding fields with cattle and sheep. The population was 5,200, about half as many again as it is today. They lived in the town's 1,500 houses and sent their children to its seven schools. Overall, the town was reasonably prosperous and underpinned the local economy. It was also important geographically.

Lying on the northwestern edge of the Santerre, a great agricultural plateau, Villers-Bretonneux bars the way to Amiens, whose urban sprawl and famous cathedral can be seen from it. The railway from

The *mairie* in prewar Villers-Bretonneux.

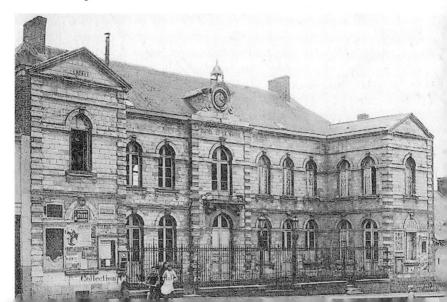

Villers-Bretonneux across the hollow from the Australian National Memorial.

Tergnier and the N29 from St Quentin, which follows the ruler-straight route of the old Roman Road, both run through the town to the city. They skirt en route three woods, the Bois d'Aquenne and the Bois de Blangy, which abut the eastern and western sides respectively of the larger Bois l'Abbé. Two miles northwards, the plateau gradually descends 200 feet to the Somme, where the villages of Hamelet, Fouilloy and Aubigny are strung out along the southern bank. Corbie is on the far side.

Hill 104, the highest part of the plateau, rises gently three quarters of a mile northeast of Villers-Bretonneux. The Australian National Memorial crowns its stubby western spur, separated by a yawning re-entrant, or hollow, from the town. Extending two miles northeastwards, its main spur peters out at Hamel below what the Germans called the Wolfsberg, which stands at the end of a parallel spur that meets the plateau at the conjoined mass of Hamel/Vaire Woods and, further east, Accroche/Arquaire Woods. Like the woods, the villages of Lamotte-Warfusée (formerly separate entities) on the N29 and Marcelcave on the railway, both three miles distant, are visible from the town's eastern edge.

The broadest part of the plateau is on the southern side of Villers-Bretonneux, which is also girded by a hollow. Cachy lies two miles southwest, with another village, Gentelles, a little beyond it. The Ferme de la Couture, a chateau set in an apple orchard in 1918, when it was known as Monument Farm, lies due south on the D23 midway between the railway and the A29 autoroute. Monument Wood, which was over the road and the larger part of the orchard, is no more, but the Bois de Morgemont and Hangard Wood East and West still stretch left and right of the D23 further south. About a mile past them, the D23 enters Démuin on the Luce, a streamlet that flows westward to the Avre past Hangard and Domart.

'Altogether it was a delightful setting for anything but grim war', wrote Ralph Keegan, an Australian gunner. But conflict had often visited Villers-Bretonneux. Henry V passed through on his way to

14

Agincourt in 1415 and sixty years later it was caught up in Louis XI's campaign to bring the Duke of Burgundy to heel. The Spanish torched it on 13 August 1636, just before they took Corbie during the Thirty Years' War, and in 1815 it was razed again in the invasion of Napoleonic France. On 27 November 1870, during the Franco-Prussian War, 7,000 French troops on the edge of the town gave General Manteufel's First Army a sharp knock as it advanced on Amiens, for which the Germans imposed a punitive levy of 100,000 francs. Now long gone, a monument commemorating the battle stood opposite the Ferme de la Couture and gave both the farm and its little wood their 1914-18 names.[1]

The town seemed to be more fortunate in that war. When stalemate settled on the Western Front at the end of 1914, Villers-Bretonneux was thirteen miles behind the line. The 1916 Somme campaign did not touch it and the German retirement to the Hindenburg Line at the start of 1917 took the fighting almost twenty miles further away. The town had also been in the French sector until the British Expeditionary Force (BEF) extended twenty-five miles southwards to the River Oise in January 1918. General Sir Hubert Gough, whose Fifth Army took over the new line, set up his headquarters in the Delacour chateau, an opulent mansion on the Roman Road that was dubbed the 'red château' because of its brickwork. Other headquarters used the less salubrious 'white château' on the town square.

The Gathering Storm
Hanging in the air was the likelihood of an all-out German offensive in the spring. The Germans knew that they had to strike a knockout blow before the American build-up in France tilted the balance decisively against them. Divisions freed up by Russia's collapse created the necessary numerical superiority. General

General Sir Hubert Gough.

Ludendorff, the First Quartermaster-General and *de facto* commander-in-chief, chose to use his new-found strength to smash the BEF, which he thought would cause the French to crumple, by attacking on the fifty-mile front between Croisilles, near Arras, and La Fère on the Oise.

Advancing towards Bapaume and Péronne respectively, the Seventeenth Army on the right and Second Army in the centre would then cross the old Somme battlefield and swing northwest on the line Arras-Albert, enveloping Arras and rolling up the BEF, which was to be driven back towards the Channel. As well as protecting the left flank, the Eighteenth Army would 'attract to itself the French reserves earmarked for the support of the British, defeat them, and sever the connection between the French and the British'. Part of the blow would fall on the shoulder of the BEF's Third Army, whose fourteen divisions held twenty-eight miles of front, including the Arras sector. Holding a forty-two-mile front with fifteen divisions, the Fifth Army stood in the way of the main thrust.[2]

Gough's line was as dilapidated as it was long, not least because the French, following a live and let live policy and knowing that they would be leaving anyway, had neglected the sector taken over from them. Though most of the BEF's labour force, 48,000 men, went to the Fifth Army, 'Nothing short of a fairy wand could have done the necessary work in time', Gough wrote later. Long stretches of its front system were either unfinished or just spitlocked in the dirt.[3]

General Ludendorff.

One other system was so far back that farmers were filling it in. Known as the Amiens Defence Line, it had been built by the French in 1915 to protect the city. The outer line ran seven miles east of Villers-Bretonneux but the Inner Line was four miles closer and linked Ribemont on the Ancre to Démuin. Crossing the Somme at Sailly-le-Sec, it seamed the Wolfsberg, where its trenches surround the Australian Corps Memorial site today, and Arquaire Wood before

Accroche/Arquaire Wood   Hamel Wood

Trench remains in the Australian Corps Memorial Park on the Wolfsberg.

going over the Roman Road 500 yards short of Warfusée-Abancourt and passing Marcelcave. Though Ludendorff did not intend initially to strike at Amiens, its importance as a railway centre and to the BEF's logistics chain made the British think differently. Its defence system entered Gough's calculations. He stopped the farmers but lacked the resources to refurbish, let alone man it.

Nevertheless, Villers-Bretonneux was so far behind the front line that only a massive breakthrough could threaten it, an unlikely prospect if past experience was any guide. British and French offensives had gained about a mile a month and never looked like breaking through. As if to make the point, Gough moved his headquarters nineteen miles eastwards to Nesle to be closer to the action. The two airfields with their canvas covered hangars alongside the Roman Road 1,000 yards east of Villers-Bretonneux smacked of a safe rear area, an impression reinforced by the untouched town. But its luck had run out.

One of the hangars on the airfields alongside the Roman Road.

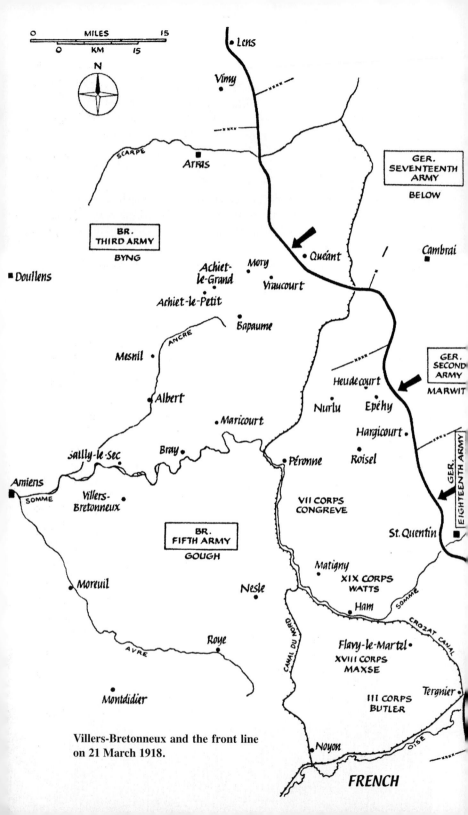

Villers-Bretonneux and the front line
on 21 March 1918.

The Storm Breaks

When Operation *Michael* broke on 21 March, the right of the Third Army was pushed back but the Fifth Army rapidly crumbled. The Germans crashed through III Corps above the Oise and Gough ordered it behind the Crozat Canal, east of the Somme. Next day, neighbouring XVIII Corps retired over the river, leaving XIX Corps on the far side. A gap opened between it and VII Corps, which was trying to stay in touch with the Third Army's right. Shoved off the Crozat Canal on 23 March, III Corps came under the French Third Army, which had joined the battle alongside it. On XVIII Corps' front, the Germans crossed the Somme, necessitating another withdrawal that also involved VII and XIX Corps. Gough's headquarters returned to Villers-Bretonneux.

At the same time, decisions taken by Ludendorff heightened the chances of the battle engulfing the town. Contrasting the twelve-mile advance in the south with the disappointing progress in the north, he shifted the weight of the attack leftwards. The Seventeenth Army would drive northwest through Arras towards Abbeville, while the Second Army advanced astride the Somme towards Amiens and the Eighteenth Army pushed the French southwest towards Noyon. Instead of the all-enveloping northwestern wheel, the three armies 'were now to sprout forth in different directions like the leaves of a fleur-de-lys'.[4]

Worried about the threat to Amiens, the BEF's Commander-in-Chief, Field Marshal Sir Douglas Haig, asked his French counterpart, General Henri Pétain, to concentrate twenty divisions near it, whereupon Pétain promised to form a Reserve Army comprising the French Third Army and a new First Army under General Debeney, with General Fayolle in overall charge. Fayolle, who would also take command of the Fifth Army south of Péronne, was to halt the Germans in front of the Canal du Nord between Nesle and Noyon. To facilitate matters, Haig made the Somme the boundary between the Third and

Operation *Michael*. The Germans attack.

Field Marshal Sir Douglas Haig.

General Henri Pétain.

Fifth Armies, which required the transfer of VII Corps on the northern side to the Third Army. But the line of the Canal du Nord went next day, 24 April. By then, the right flank had gone back seventeen miles, whereas the Arras flank had barely budged.

The Germans now had to contend with the shattered ground of the 1916 Somme campaign. Their artillery and logistics could not keep up and the Second Army's progress astride the river stalled. As the Eighteenth Army was still advancing rapidly against the French Third Army south of Nesle, Ludendorff modified the plan again on 25 March. While the Second Army continued to advance on Amiens, the Eighteeenth was to strengthen its own right wing so that, in conjunction with the Second Army, it might gain the line from the Avre to Caix, six miles southeast of Villers-Bretonneux. The Seventeenth

Troops from III Corps fight alongside the French near Nesle on 25 March 1918.

Army would launch Operation *Mars* to 'shake and smash' the British around Arras on 28 March, with Operation *Georgette* to follow on the Lys.

On the battlefield on 25 March, VII Corps north of the Somme occupied a line from the edge of Albert to Bray, nine miles northeast of Villers-Bretonneux. The left of XIX Corps was four miles further east at Frise on the southern bank, from which the 16th (Irish) Division, under a brigade strong, stretched rearwards to protect the Fifth Army's flank. Gough moved his headquarters to Dury, south of Amiens. With the Germans now less than twenty miles from the city, he looked to the Amiens Defence Line as a backstop and culled his headquarters and the rear area for men to work on and garrison its inner line:

> . . . *electrical and mechanical engineers, surveyors – 500 men of the U.S. Engineers – tunnellers and miners – Army, Corps and Sniping Schools – signallers. The Army Signal School supplied communications, 9 grooms acted as mounted orderlies . . . The total strength of the force amounted to just over 2,000 men.*[5]

Brigadier-General G.G.S. Carey took command of what became known as Carey's Force and set up its headquarters in Villers-Bretonneux. Lieutenant General Sir Herbert Watts, the commander of XIX Corps, was also there. Other men were scraped together to start a reserve line west of the town. Running northwards from Fouencamps on the Avre, it touched the eastern side of Gentelles, passed behind Cachy and swung northeast through the Bois l'Abbé before crossing the Roman Road and the railway line in O.26.d on its way to Aubigny. The system was known as the Gentelles Line below the Roman Road and the Aubigny Line above it.

Covering Amiens
Meanwhile, tensions were growing between Haig and Pétain. Haig was relying on the French to support his right while the Third Army held onto Arras. For Pétain, a withdrawal pivoting on Arras meant that the BEF was retreating northwest, which amounted, he told Haig on 24 April, to 'withdraw[ing] your hand in proportion as I'm stretching mine out to you'. With the Fifth Army stuck in reverse gear, sending it more help was like throwing good money after bad at a time when the French themselves were about to be heavily attacked. If the German drive towards Amiens continued, Pétain said, Fayolle was to abandon the BEF's right flank and fall back southwestwards to cover Paris.

Haig was thunderstruck. Amiens loomed large as British and French

General (later Marshal) Ferdinand Foch.

military and political leaders met at his instigation on 26 March at Doullens. Writing off the Fifth Army, Pétain remarked: 'It no longer exists, it is broken'. Amiens was therefore wide open, whereupon General Ferdinand Foch, Chairman of the Allied Executive War Board at Versailles, interjected:

We must fight in front of Amiens, we must fight where we are now. As we have not been able to stop the Germans on the Somme, we must not now retire a single inch.

Appointed to co-ordinate the operations of both allies, Foch took what he had said as his guiding principles: 'Before everything else, the French and British troops, remaining closely in touch, must cover Amiens . . . To this end, the troops already engaged must hold their ground'. Strong reinforcements were to be sent to Fayolle, who was directed to relieve the Fifth Army up to the Somme.[6]

During the meeting, XIX Corps, the only part of the Fifth Army still under Gough's command, eliminated its exposed left flank on the Somme by pulling back to Froissy, opposite Bray. Gough thought that the Germans were becoming 'worn out and very tired'. Ironically, given the French accusations against the Fifth Army, the only place where the Germans still found the going easy was on their front, where the Eighteenth Army drove the French Third Army back nine miles. But then a crisis flared on the Somme to threaten the British front and bring the battle to the very edge of Villers-Bretonneux.

NOTES

1. Extracts from Archives Départementales de la Somme, *Monographies des Communes de France: Villers-Bretonneux,* (4 pages, 1899); R.M. Keegan, 'An Even Break', MSS 1333, Australian War Memorial (AWM).
2. J.E. Edmonds, *Military Operations: France and Belgium, 1918. I. The German March Offensive* (Macmillan, 1935), p. 149. Hereafter *Military Operations I.*
3. H. Gough, *The Fifth Army* (Hodder & Stoughton, 1931), p. 225.
4. G. Blaxland, *Amiens 1918* (Star, 1981), p. 69.
5. Gough, op. cit., pp. 299-300.
6. B. Pitt, 1918 *The Last Act* (Papermac, 1984), p. 95; *Military Operations I,* pp. 541-2; C. Barnett, *The Swordbearers,* (Papermac, 1986), p. 326.

Chapter Two

EARLY ENCOUNTERS

Soon after the Doullens conference, Haig was embarrassed to learn that VII Corps had abandoned Bray and swung behind the Ancre, leaving the triangle of ground between it and the Somme virtually undefended. The corps commander, Lieutenant General Sir William Congreve VC, had misinterpreted an earlier order to retire only if 'the tactical situation imperatively demands it' as a direction to fall back regardless. Now nothing but a scratch force of infantry and cavalry in the old Amiens Defence Line, screened by 2 Cavalry Brigade, stretched across the triangle from the Ancre to Sailly-le-Sec on the Somme.

The calamity brought the Australian 3rd, 4th and 5th Divisions, which Haig had just switched to his reserve, southwards. While the 4th Division secured the high ground on the Ancre, the 3rd Division took

The gap opened up by the mistaken retirement of VII Corps on the Somme on 26 March 1918.

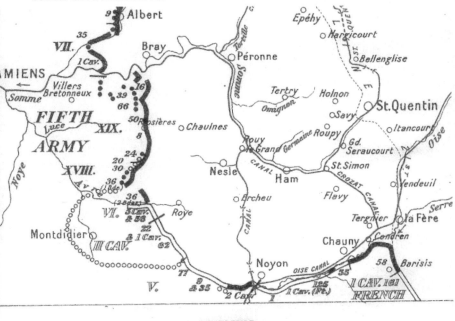

over the Amiens Defence Line in the triangle. It was to pay particular attention to the Somme flank, now six miles behind the Fifth Army's left opposite Bray. Should the Germans jump the Somme in this gap, they could outflank the Fifth Army and then continue on the southern side of the river before recrossing to turn the right flank of the Third Army. In that case, their faltering offensive would have a clear run to Amiens through the rear areas of both armies. That evening, Ludendorff ordered the Second Army to press forward with its left on Moreuil, a town on the Avre twelve miles south east of Amiens, while its centre captured Amiens itself.

Crossing the Somme
On the left of the Second Army's advance between the Somme and the Ancre on 27 March, 1 Grenadier Regiment and 43 Infantry Regiment (IR) of XIV Corps' 1st Division sought to cross to the southern bank of the Somme between Sailly-le-Sec and Sailly-Laurette, a mile further east, at 9.30 am. The 3rd Australian Division in the Amiens Defence

The German crossing of the Somme on 27 March 1918 and the subsequent advance.

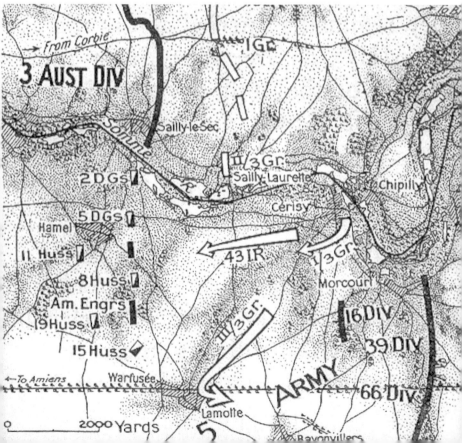

III/3 Grenadier's advance from Cerisy.

Line watched the cavalry in the screen ahead holding them off throughout the day. Four squadrons from 4 and 5/Dragoon Guards even occupied Sailly-Laurette and withstood attacks from three sides. Blocked up front, 43 IR switched its effort to Cerisy, a mile short of Sailly-Laurette and four and a half miles behind the left of XIX Corps on the river. Eighty sappers from the 16th (Irish) Division put up a dour fight at Cerisy's partly destroyed bridge but the Germans were over by 2 pm.

Next, two engineer companies from Carey's Force were pushed off Hill 66, which overlooks the village from the southwest. According to Gough, they 'had received no training as soldiers and could hardly handle a rifle'.[1] But enough time had been gained for 400 stragglers to be collected at Lamotte and organised for a counterattack. Launched at 4 pm, it reached the small wood at Q.14.b, which commanded the exits from Cerisy, 1,500 yards northeastwards, an hour later. By then, 3 Battalion from Major von Johnston's 3 Grenadier Regiment had reinforced the left of 43 IR, giving the Germans four battalions in the bridgehead. Von Johnston ordered it to ignore its flanks and head

Lamotte in ruins.

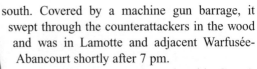

south. Covered by a machine gun barrage, it swept through the counterattackers in the wood and was in Lamotte and adjacent Warfusée-Abancourt shortly after 7 pm.

Unwilling to counterattack with Carey's Force, which in any case was all that stood between Villers-Bretonneux and the Germans, and with the rest of XIX Corps still fighting the main battle to the east, Gough had been very relieved to find out at 5.30 pm that Fayolle was returning XVIII Corps to the Fifth Army. He gave the 61st Division, the first to leave, to XIX Corps and had it transported to Marcelcave for a counterattack on Lamotte, one and a half miles

General Sir Henry Rawlinson. northeast, at 5 am next morning. The Third Army had already sent him the 1st Cavalry Division, which would beef up the sector most threatened: the Amiens Inner Line from the river through the Wolfsberg to the Roman Road. In order to protect the Third Army's right flank if the Germans punched through, the 3rd Australian Division's reserve, Brigadier General Charles Rosenthal's 9 Brigade, deployed to guard the Somme crossings between Sailly-le-Sec and Aubigny.

In the midst of these developments, Gough learned that he was to be relieved. He had a reputation for callousness and, with the Fifth Army badly mauled, became the scapegoat that the British retirement since 21 March demanded. General Sir Henry Rawlinson, who had commanded the Fourth Army on the Somme in 1916 and was currently the British Military Representative on the Allied Executive War Board, would succeed him. Gough had no time to brood because the Germans now had at least 2,000 men behind XIX Corps. Warned by Watts that a withdrawal was the only way of preventing its envelopment, Gough had Foch woken at 3 am on 28 March and got his consent for XIX Corps to wheel back through Caix to link up with Carey's Force at Marcelcave, four miles northwest. The Australian Official Historian, C.E.W. Bean, remarked of the Fifth Army up to that point:

> Far from being 'non-existent', as Pétain believed, they maintained in very hard fighting, throughout the 27th and until the morning of the 28th, a line not far short of that which Foch on March 26th had ordered them to hold.[2]

The French, on the other hand, had withdrawn twenty miles since Foch issued his 'no retreat' order at Doullens. On 27 March, a nine-mile gap

26

opened up between their First and Second Armies, which allowed the Germans to enter Montdidier, like Amiens, an important railway centre.

Getting Closer

The 61st Division's counterattack on Lamotte went in while XIX Corps was coming back. By 1918, the 61st, a second line territorial formation, 'reckoned it had been unlucky at everything it had attempted and called itself the Sixty-worst'.[3] Its virtual destruction during the retreat showed its luck had not changed. 183 and 184 Brigades, the rump formations detailed for the operation, were so tired that their commanders chose to rest them by attacking at noon on 28 March instead of dawn as Gough had wanted. But the plan did not lend itself to being executed in daylight. Though the railway cutting on the northern edge of Marcelcave offered the attackers a covered start line, ahead of them, on the axis of the modern D42, lay an open assault of 2,500 yards, over which the Germans had unbroken fields of fire. They had also been ensconced in Warfusée-Abancourt and Lamotte for eighteen hours.

As soon as the two brigades were in range, the German machine guns opened. Incredibly, the counterattack still got to within 200 yards of the villages. With no hope of further progress, it was abandoned at 3.40 pm and the survivors retired to the railway cutting. Capitalising on the failure, the Germans struck Marcelcave at 6 pm. Carey's garrison buckled under the terrific preparatory bombardment and the men on either side of the village retreated as well, resulting in the collapse of the central sector of the line. Watts, who had prudently moved his headquarters to St Fuscien, near the Fifth Army's headquarters at Dury, sent up his last reserve, the corps signal company. But the hole had already been plugged because 183 and 184 Brigades had withdrawn from the railway and dug in half a mile west of Marcelcave when they saw the Germans getting behind them.

Earlier, at 4 pm, the German 1st Division and the 4th Guards Division, also from XIV Corps, tried to seize both Hamel and the main spur running from it to Hill 104. 2/(Queen's Bays) and 5/Dragoon Guards of 1 Cavalry Brigade, the remnants of the 16th (Irish) Division,

The 61st Division's counterattack on Lamotte. Marcelcave, from whence it started, is on the far side of the A29 autoroute.

Marcelcave church at war's end.

and the usual hotchpotch from Carey's Force faced them. Their machine guns and the artillery ripped into 43 IR and I/3 Grenadiers as they crested the steep western slope of the Vallée d'Abancourt in front. British aircraft prevented ammunition reaching the guns the Germans had brought up. Their attack recoiled and 5 Guard Grenadiers were thrown in to kickstart it. They had no success either.

German attacks elsewhere were roughly handled as well. Operation *Mars*, which was supposed to prise open the Third Army's line at Arras, 'turned out to be just another classic Western Front offensive . . By the end of the day the Germans had failed to gain a single lodgement in the British battle zone'.[4] On the opposite flank, a counterattack by the French Third Army drove the stunned Germans back a couple of miles towards Montdidier. When Rawlinson formally succeeded Gough at 4.30 pm on 28 March, the Anglo-French front was solid everywhere except between the Somme and the Avre.

Struggling On

Calling Watts that morning to find out how things were going, Rawlinson was told: 'They may well get us by lunch-time and you by tea-time'. When he read Gough's brief on the state of the Fifth Army, Rawlinon might well have wondered whether Watts was not kidding. Its infantry strength was 21,650, of which 8,000 were in III Corps, still with the French. The 8th, 30th and 50th Divisions were estimated to have a fighting strength of 'perhaps 2,000' men each, while the 66th was down to 500. Those in XVIII Corps were graded 'unreliable' to varying degrees except for the 1,500-strong 61st, which was 'all but tired out' and 'unfit to counterattack'.[5] Writing to Foch on taking command, Rawlinson warned:

> The situation is serious, and unless fresh troops are sent here in the next two days, I doubt whether the remnants of the British XIX Corps which now hold the line to the east of Villers-Bretonneux can maintain their positions. . .
>
> I feel some anxiety for the security of Amiens, and draw your attention to the danger in which this place will be if the enemy renews his attacks from the east before fresh troops are available. I fear that the troops of the XIX Corps are not capable of executing a counteroffensive.[6]

Foch could do little beyond cajole, entreat and promise. As the fragile front around Montdidier would soak up incoming French divisions, he was unable to relieve the Fifth Army. On the contrary, he told Haig on 29 March, it would not only have to reorganise *in situ* and struggle on as best it could, but would also have to extend its line southwards from its existing flank at Démuin on the Luce to Moreuil on the Avre. At least the French were returning III Corps and the 2nd and 3rd Cavalry Divisions, which had been operating with it as mounted infantry for much of the time.

Neverthless, Rawlinson was taking over more of the only front that still held out any prospect of success for the Germans after their mauling on 28 March. They drove the French beyond Démuin next day, necessitating a counterattack by 20th Division from XVIII Corps, which secured a line between Démuin and Moreuil Wood that almost amounted to the extra stretch allocated by Foch. The only attack on the Fifth Army's sector breached the line on the southern shoulder of the Wolfsberg, prompting a callout of 11/Hussars from their support position in rear. Seeing the cavalrymen dismount 300 yards away, fix bayonets and start up the slope, the Germans bolted without a fight. Worried about the danger to Rawlinson's extended flank, Haig sent 9 Australian Brigade to Cachy, where it was to come under the 61st Division for use in counterattacks. 15 Brigade from the 5th Australian Division replaced it on the Somme crossings.

Realising that Operation *Michael* was all but dead, Ludendorff ordered the Sixth Army to mount *Georgette* on the Lys, weather permitting, within ten days. At the same time, he was too close to Amiens to resist trying to grab it, even if the attempt achieved no more than bringing its railway complex under artillery fire. *Michael's* grandiose objectives had dwindled to a face-saving local operation to capture a railway centre. The Germans wrote of the operations for 30 March:

> *Amiens is now the objective; to secure that place all the efforts of this and the following days will be directed; the attacks near Montdidier and eastward of that town are only diversions designed to detain the enemy forces.[7]*

The Second Army's left wing and the Eighteenth Army's right were to take the shortest route towards Amiens, advancing either side of the Avre in a northwesterly direction. From Sailly-Laurette to the right of the French Third Army at Noyon, the attack frontage was twenty-five miles.

Lancer Wood

Covered by low-flying aircraft after an eighty-minute bombardment, eight German divisions assaulted the Fifth Army's line north of Moreuil. The 20th Division lost Démuin, enabling the 208th Division to enfilade Aubercourt on the other side of the Luce. Its fire helped the 19th Division's 91 IR force the 66th Division out of the village and towards Hangard Wood, Hangard and the Bois de Morgemont on the next spur west. The 39th Division alongside it also went back. Severely shelled, the remnants of the 61st Division further north swung their line opposite Marcelcave towards the Roman Road. A German drive up the Luce Valley, which would outflank Villers-Bretonneux, was now a very real danger. At 12.30 pm on 30 March, Watts wrote afterwards,

> *As it was clear that some of the depleted divisions now in the line were not really in a fit state for further action, and could not be trusted to maintain their positions against enemy pressure, I decided to employ the 9th Australian Brigade to counterattack southeast to restore the situation about Aubercourt.*

Completing its move from the Somme at 4 am, 9 Brigade had assembled in the Bois l'Abbé because Cachy, its original destination, attracted heavy shelling. Brigadier General Charles Rosenthal set up his headquarters near the 61st Division's in Gentelles at the insistence of its commander, Major General Colin Mackenzie, under whose authority he came, but commanded from a brigade report centre in the wood at O.33.c.3.4. At 11 am, he was ordered to 'resist the supposed advance of enemy' by securing the Villers-Bretonneux-Cachy-Domart Road. 9 Brigade's War Diary commented: 'This order was not complied with as the role of the Brigade is one of counterattack'.

Watts's 12.30 pm order was more appropriate: 'an attack against the line MARCELCAVE-AUBERCOURT this afternoon' to 'clear up situation as regards position and nature of our front line'. At 2.10 pm, Rosenthal met Lieutenant Colonel Leslie Morshead, the commander of 33 Battalion, in the brigade report centre and told him to take up a line three and a half miles eastwards that stretched 2,700 yards from V.9.a.2.0, a copse 1,000 yards short of Marcelcave on the left, to Aubercourt and, if possible, Démuin on the right. A twenty-eight year-old former schoolteacher who had landed at Gallipoli and would command Tobruk during the famous siege in the next war, Morshead asked a question that started a curt exchange:

Brigadier General Charles Rosenthal.

> *When are we to do it? Now.*
> *Any artillery? No.*
> *Do you know where the British line is?*
> *No* (hence the lack of artillery support).[8]

As the 500 men in 33 Battalion amounted to less than one man per five yards of the objective line, 34 Battalion would support the attack but Morshead was not to use it unless absolutely necessary. The 400-strong 12/Lancers from the newly arrived 2nd Cavalry Division's 5 Brigade would also assist.

At 3.10 pm, the two battalions, with the 33rd leading and the cavalry drawing ahead, began the march to the assembly area on the western side of the Villers-Bretonneux-Démuin Road, today's D23, opposite the Bois de Morgemont. For Private John Hardie in B Company of the 33rd,

> *It was a lovely sight. Our great*

Lieutenant Colonel Leslie Morshead.

31

long columns of Infantry in battle order and the Lancers riding alongside in their squares with gleaming lances and swords. It was just like some of the scenes I have read about of troops going into battle.

Passing south of Villers-Bretonneux and the northern tip of Hangard Wood East, they reached the Bois de Morgemont about 4.35 pm amidst large parties of stragglers, and bodies of men 'peculiarly and uselessly entrenched in queer places'. By then 12/Lancers on its own initiative had secured the Bois de Morgemont after driving advanced parties of Germans from its southern and eastern edges. Morshead wrote subsequently:

It was a proud privilege to work with such a fine regiment as 12 Lancers. Their approach march instilled in the men the utmost confidence and enthusiasm, and I am glad to say greatly counteracted the effect of so much straggling.

At his recommendation, the British called the Bois de Morgemont Lancer Wood thereafter.

33 Battalion advanced towards the wood in drizzling rain at 5 pm with three companies in line and the fourth, C Company, remaining on the D23 in reserve. The attack went smoothly until it was 200 yards clear of the wood, when the Australians came into view of 91 IR. This regiment occupied the line formerly held by the 39th and 66th Divisions along the crest of the spur that runs down to Aubercourt, crowned now by Toronto Cemetery. Reserve battalions from 78 IR had also been rushed up to strengthen it. With no barrage to suppress them, the Germans raked the advance with deadly accurate fire, particularly from the southern flank, which was enfiladed by III/91 IR. 'The boys started to drop all around, slowly at first but quicker as we got closer' Hardie recalled. 'I kept watching the little puffs of steam the red hot bullets made in the sodden fields'.

The Australians immediately launched a bayonet charge under the inadequate covering fire of their own machine guns. Tasked with capturing Aubercourt, D Company on the right was soon stopped, while A Company in the centre barely advanced past it. Only B Company on the left got close to its objective opposite Marcelcave, at one stage throwing I/78 IR back 350 yards. With 300 men holding a

Looking south at the ground over which 33 Battalion and 12/Lancers attacked Lancer Wood.

Lancer Wood   Hangard Wood East   Hangard Wood We

12/Lance

33 & 34 Bns

D23

The attack on Lancer Wood.

gap-riddled line almost a mile long as night fell, Morshead ordered C Company into the largest gap, which had opened between A and D Companies, and called on 34 Battalion to fill the others. In one of the most dramatic episodes of the battle, one of its companies swept between A and B Companies of the 33rd to capture the German line 250 yards beyond them before withdrawing. Hardie again:

> The enemy screamed and howled for mercy but all he got was the bayonet, that is, those that didn't run away. Our lads didn't fire a shot but used the bayonet something awful . . . they [had] passed over our wounded and dying coming up and it roused their blood.

While the Australian positions in the low ground were difficult for the Germans to discern against the background of Lancer Wood in the darkness, the German line was plainly silhouetted on the crest despite the drenching rain. When the Germans massed for a counterattack at 11 pm, B Company saw them 'right away along the skyline about 300 yards away. Well we opened up and in less than no time there wasn't a Hun showing'. Though the breach was sealed, Aubercourt remained a mile distant and the Germans still held their newly captured positions. Of the 200 Australian casualties, 33 Battalion suffered 168. 12/Lancers, whose machine guns had protected the flanks of the attack, lost fifteen men.[9]

North and South

The 4th Guards and 228th Divisions of XIV Corps attacked between the Roman Road and the Somme at 1 pm on 30 March. The 228th was completely fresh and, on hearing the cocks crowing in Hamel the night before, confidently predicted: 'We'll have you in the pot tomorrow'. Untroubled by the bombardment, the British machine guns traversed along the German line as it advanced across the Wolfsberg towards them. The attack stalled except in the centre, where it entered Hamel after breaking through 48 and 49 Brigades of the 16th (Irish) Division,

The line reached by the Australians at Lancer Wood.

Hangard Wood East   Lancer Wood

Australian Line

Tired British cavalry in Corbie after the fighting on 30 March 1918.

so weak that they had been formed into composite battalions.
5/Dragoon Guards in support rallied them and ejected the Germans,
who 'left many dead on the wire'. The 228th Division's 35 Fusilier
Regiment suffered its heaviest losses of the war. Closer to the road, the
machine gun fire was so intense that the 4th Guards could not get to
the line of departure. Its 5 Grenadier Regiment, which had assaulted
there two days before, needed immediate relief.[10]

German attacks north of the Somme were also roughly handled. In fact, the only real drama arose on the southern flank, where fighting swayed to and fro across Rifle and Little Woods, both above the Luce on the D23, before the 20th and 50th Divisions finally recaptured them. Further south, the French abandoned Moreuil Wood but a counterattack by the Canadian Cavalry Brigade, commanded by Brigadier General 'Galloper Jack' Seely, a former British Secretary of State for War, recovered the bulk of it, after which the 8th Division relieved the cavalry on a line that ran to the western side of Moreuil. Though not in the manner intended, the Fifth Army's right was now on the inter-allied boundary Foch had stipulated. The rest of the French line either retired only a short distance or stopped the Germans cold.

The day's outcome was a major disappointment for Ludendorff. But he could not let go of Amiens and an advance south of the Somme by the Second and Eighteenth Armies still offered the best chance of getting it. He agreed to a pause first. Besides allowing his tired divisions to rest, it would also enable the roads to be repaired so that enough ammunition could be brought up for an annihilating bombardment prior to the attack. This was fixed for 4 April. In the only significant operation beforehand, the Germans tried to straighten the line around Moreuil Wood on 31 March. The 8th Division's 25 Brigade, 200 strong, recaptured the wood's northern offshoot and, on 1 April, the 2nd Cavalry Division and the Canadian Cavalry Brigade regained most of the ground lost north of it.

NOTES

1. Gough, op. cit., p. 314.
2. C.E.W. Bean, *The Official History of Australia in the War of 1914-1918. V. The AIF in France During The Main German Offensive, 1918* (Angus & Robertson, 1941), p. 277. Hereafter *OH*.
3. M. Middlebrook, *The Kaiser's Battle* (Allen Lane, 1978), p. 92.
4. C. Barnett, 'Offensive 1918' in N. Frankland & C. Dowling (eds), *Decisive Battles of the Twentieth Century* (Hutchinson, 1976), pp. 78-9.
5. Gough's report quoted in Blaxland, op. cit., pp. 98-100.
6. J.E. Edmonds, *Military Operations: France and Belgium, 1918. II. March-April: Continuation of the German Offensives* (Macmillan, 1937), p. 51. Hereafter *Military Operations II*.
7. Ibid, p. 87.
8. *OH*, pp. 299, 302; 9 Bde WD, 30 March 1918, Item 23/9, Roll 18, AWM 4.
9. Hardie to parents, 24 April 1918, PR00519, AWM; 33 Bn Counterattack Report, 31 March 1918, Appendix 19 to 9 Bde WD, Item 23/9, Roll 18, AWM 4; 12 Lancers WD, 30 March 1918, WO 95/1140, TNA; *OH*, p. 307.
10. *OH*, p. 294; C.E.W. Bean, *Anzac to Amiens* (AWM, 1968), p. 420; 5 Dragoon Guards WD, 30 March 1918, WO 95/1109, TNA.

Chapter Three

THE LULL

The first phase of the defence of Villers-Bretonneux ended with the Germans contained in front of the town. While the infantry divisions played their part, the cavalry had been instrumental in keeping them at bay. As it largely escaped the attritional battles that had emasculated most infantry divisions by the end of 1917, the cavalry could draw on the skill and experience of a higher proportion of surviving regulars. But its pool of trained replacements was nearly empty. Nor were fresh infantry divisions available. So Rawlinson had to relieve the exhausted formations of XIX Corps with the 14th (Light), 18th (Eastern) and 58th Divisions of III Corps, which Fayolle had begun sending back on 28 March. General Watts would hand over to the corps commander, Lieutenant General Sir Richard Butler, when their arrival was complete.

III Corps

In terms of their fitness for action, the incoming formations were hardly a great advance over the outgoing ones. All three had been in the front line when the Germans attacked and, in the week that followed, the 14th Division sustained 3,197 casualties, the 18th 2,445 and the 58th 832. Their few days' respite with the French since was spent in reserve or support rather than actual rest. Despite receiving some replacement drafts, they remained understrength, especially in officers and trained NCOs. Without them and with no real chance to refit and retrain, absorbing and training the new arrivals properly was impossible. The 18th Division History remarked that its 'fresh recruits, most of them raw youths', were denied the opportunity to 'become imbued with the corporate spirit of the Division'.[1]

The 18th Division was a New Army formation. Under Major

Cavalry in action during the March Offensive.

General Ivor Maxse, one of the great tacticians and trainers of his generation, it was 'arguably the most consistently successful British division in the 1916 Somme offensive' it had captured the hitherto impregnable fortress of Thiepval.[2] When Maxse left to command XVIII Corps in January 1917, the Fifth Army's Chief Engineer, Major General Richard Lee, took over. Brigadier Generals H.W. Higginson and L.W. de V. Sadleir-Jackson commanded 53 and 54 Brigades respectively. 'Short, stout and with a boozer's complexion', Brigadier General Edward Wood led 55 Brigade. Dropping his age from forty-nine to forty-two to command a company at the

Major General Richard Lee.

start of the war, he had won four DSOs, nine Mentions in Despatches, been wounded five times, gassed twice and buried once by war's end. Private Robert Cude of 7/Buffs, a cynical veteran who was one of Wood's runners, swore that 'as long as he stops at Brigade, I shall not mind going through hell itself'.[3]

53 and 55 Brigades began arriving in the Gentelles Line on 29 March. Along with the divisional advanced headquarters, Captain R. Chell of 10/Essex was billeted in the village:

Brigadier General Edward Wood *(Shropshire Regimental Museum).*

There were cockerels crowing, hens cackling, and pigs snorting, alarmed at the unusual tramp of feet. Hunger had been hard to bear, but here was the reward. Next day we gorged on fowl and pig. So lavishly did we feed on these that for long afterwards the sight of feathered fowl and bristled beast awakened the feelings of a sea voyage![4]

Chell's gratification did not last long. On 30 March, Watts directed the two formations to relieve the 66th, 39th and 61st Divisions between the Luce and the Roman Road that night. They were in position next morning. 10/Essex took over from Morshead's Australians, who resumed their role as counterattack troops.

Arriving later in the day, 54 Brigade was the first to see action when, on 2 April, a company from both 11/Royal Fusiliers and 7/Bedfords attacked the high ground north of Aubercourt that had eluded Morshead's men. Catching them forming up in the trees on the northern bank of the Luce, the Germans brought down a heavy barrage and their machine guns opened up from the front and across the river. The Fusiliers quickly lost forty-two men, the Bedfords sixty-four. Supposed to join the assault at the southern tip of Lancer Wood, a company of 7/Royal West Kents was shot up when it mistook some German flares for the signal to advance. The attack was abandoned.

Consisting of 41, 42 and 43 Brigades, the 14th (Light) Division, one of the first New Army formations, arrived next. Even allowing for the fact that it was the most heavily attacked British division on 21 March, the 14th 'did not fight well. . . Its forward positions fell quickly; many men surrendered, and some hasty flights to the rear were observed'. Next day its commander, Major General Sir Victor Couper, became the first senior officer to be sacked in the battle. Butler stated that he was 'suffering from want of sleep and rest and, in my opinion, was not in a fit state to handle the situation for the time being'. In turn, Couper's replacement, Major General W.H. 'Bob' Greenly, was considered 'not fit to continue operations' by 28 March, Haig's diary stating that he 'went off his head with the strain'. Brigadier P.C.B. Skinner assumed command on 31 March, the day before the 14th Division took over the right of the Fifth Army's line.[5]

As a second line territorial formation, the 58th Division was not fully equipped until mid-1916 and only went to France in January 1917. Comprising 173, 174 and 175 Brigades, it was led by Major General A.B.E. Cator and, unlike the 14th and 18th Divisions, remained in the front line during its stay with the French. Consequently, the 58th was the last division to be released. The first units, 6 and 7/Londons from 174 Brigade, reached Amiens station on 3 April.

The Australians

If the formations of III Corps were played out by normal standards, the opposite was true of the Australians. They were at their peak. On 1 November 1917, the Australian Corps had been created, satisfying their long held desire for all five Australian divisions to be grouped

Resting Australians engaged in gambling, their favourite pastime.

together. Four months spent recuperating, refitting and training at Messines during the winter had given morale another fillip. With few casualties, the flow of returning wounded eased the manpower shortage caused by Third Ypres, and the Australians did not have to reduce the number of battalions per brigade from four to three as the British did. They were also among the first to receive extra Lewis guns when the number in each platoon was doubled.

The Australians had two intangible qualities that made them unique. In no other army did the closeness of the small group sustain its soldiers as much. With leave to Australia non-existent, home and its concerns faded to the deepest recesses of a soldier's mind. His platoon, and by extension, company and battalion, filled the void, effectively becoming his family. The result was an aggressive spirit and confidence that verged on arrogance.

Next, the Australian soldier was always a uniformed civilian, who accepted regulation as a temporary necessity rather than an all-embracing creed. His intelligence, curiosity and initiative unfettered, he was very much a soldier who reasoned why. Those qualities shone in action but out of it he was his own man and became notorious for his indiscipline, a contrast that made others ambivalent towards him. Haig seethed at the size of the Australian military prison population, proportionally ten times larger than the British in 1918, but he still counted the Australians among his best troops.

The start of the German offensive boosted the Australians' morale still higher. They knew that this battle would determine the outcome of the war and were anxious to get to the Somme to enter it. *'Fini retreat – beaucoup Australiens ici'*, the assurance they gave to French civilians on the journey south, immediately became one of the great national statements. Their high spirits and conceited indifference irritated Lieutenant P.J. Campbell, an English gunner.

During the afternoon Australian soldiers came up from behind, they went along the road past our guns, up towards the line. This was the first time I had seen Australians, they were unlike any of our own divisions, and on this first occasion I was not attracted by them. They were noisy and swaggering, they did not march along the road, they just walked, they seemed to be without any kind of discipline.

Private Cude was unequivocal: 'I hate the Aussies, as does all British Tommies'.

For their part, many Australians thought that the Tommies could not be counted upon in a tough fight. This sentiment had originated at Suvla in the Gallipoli campaign, become established after the July 1916 debacle at Fromelles, the Australians' first major battle in France, and was hardened by the scenes they witnessed at the end of March 1918 when refugees remarked, *'English soldat no bon!'*. Lancer Wood seemed to confirm the Australians' negative opinion, their fulsome praise of the cavalry notwithstanding. 'During the whole time we were forward men were constantly leaving the line. There seemed to be no effort to check this straggling', Morshead reported. The 61st Division between the railway and the Roman Road had also been very shaky, forcing Major General Mackenzie to relieve it with 35 Battalion, thereby abandoning the plan to use 9 Brigade's battalions solely for counterattacks.[6]

Temptations and Tensions

Still largely intact, Villers-Bretonneux was now virtually in the front line and its inhabitants, apart from a few old people and a mother and her children, had gone. A passing Australian, who had seen the woman stacking some belongings onto a cart, stopped, declared: 'You needn't go, Ma. The Aussies are here. Best stay where you are', and helped her carry them back into her house. Though the town had been looted during the retreat, much remained – 'beaucoup vin and champagne, poultry, tinned food and vegetables', another Australian said. Rather than let it go to waste, they helped themselves. Shivering in the sodden fields to the southeast, 35 Battalion greatly appreciated the supplementary delicacies that came up with the hot meal each night.[7]

Aware of the Australians' reputation for indiscipline, Major General Lee, under whose command they came after the 61st Division's relief, feared widespread drunkenness among them. Encountering some carrying sacks and guessing what they contained, he struck the sacks with 'a thick oak stick, and caused cascades of red and white wines to flow freely down the Australians' backs'. The 18th Division's history implies that Lee would have been beaten up but for the timely arrival of some Australian officers. Yet Lee's men, Private Cude among them, were doing the same:

> My first stunt was a bath in a shop which apparently thrived as a Perfumery, and the bath that I have is half full of Eau-de Cologne, and I take half dozen bottles to be sent home as soon as I get a chance . . . tons of canned fruit, meat, and game were stacked up ready to be eaten. In the drinking line, we have our choice of wines of all qualities and age, but our attention is drawn to the champagne that is present in large number . . . We soon have reinforcements down with stretchers, and for myself a pass signed by General [Wood] to bring away anything that I salvage. Journey after journey I make, and we have enough to last out a siege of a few weeks very soon, and then we turn our attention to the other shops and houses.[8]

On the Australian side, Brigadier General Harold 'Pompey' Elliott, the commander of 15 Brigade, did his bit for poor relations. A highly-strung giant of a man, he evinced, said Bean, 'a hot-headed tendency to use his brigade as if it were independent of the rest of the BEF'. Made up of 57, 58, 59 and 60 Battalions, it was 'at the zenith of its form; a magnificent instrument, fit, like Cromwell's Ironsides, for the hardest military tasks'. A twenty-six-mile night march to relieve 9 Brigade on the Somme crossings on 30 March was the first.

Elliott knew that if the flimsy front south of the river gave way, his brigade would be involved in a fight to the death to secure the BEF's right flank. Nor was he in any doubt that the widespread looting of liquor by British stragglers in Corbie would jeopardise the defence if it continued. As the men would not desist unless their

Brigadier General Harold Elliott.

officers did, Elliott ordered the arrest of any officer caught taking wine. The edict had no effect because a captain was subsequently arrested with his brigade mess-cart loaded with champagne. Elliott directed that 'the next officer caught looting would be summarily hanged in the Corbie market square, and his body would be left swinging there as a deterrent'. The order stopped the looting immediately. 'None seemed willing to make themselves a test case', he drily observed.[9]

Strengthening the Line

Had III Corps arrived fresh and at full strength, what soldiers call the 'troops to task' problem facing Rawlinson would still have been acute because, even with 9 Brigade added, he needed more men to hold his long line securely. On 1 April, Haig told Prime Minister Georges Clemenceau that unless the French extended across the Avre, as he had promised they would do two days earlier, the Fifth Army would be stretched too thinly to protect Villers-Bretonneux and hence Amiens. Stung, Clemenceau summoned Foch, who promptly ordered Fayolle to carry out the relief as far north as the Luce. The French came in between Moreuil and Hangard the next night, releasing the 14th

Division to relieve the 1st Cavalry Division and Whitmore's 'Cosmopolitan Force' (the remnants of Carey's Force, the 16th Division and some other cavalry) from the Roman Road to the Somme on the night of 3-4 April.

Forming part of the old Amiens Inner Line, this sector was the most established section of the Fifth Army's front. As the Wolfsberg overlooked the Vallée d'Abancourt, it was also the most defensible. With 9/Rifle Brigade and 5/Ox and Bucks on the left and right respectively, 42 Brigade extended one and a half miles from Bouzencourt on the river to Arquaire Wood. 7 and 8/Rifle Brigades of 41 Brigade covered the same distance from there to the Roman Road. 43 Brigade was in reserve on Hill 104. Worried by the 14th Division's lack of numbers and its brittleness, especially since the division had been involved in reliefs on the two previous nights and was more tired now than when it arrived, General Watts put 6 Cavalry Brigade from the 3rd Cavalry Division in reserve behind it and told the outgoing cavalry to leave their machine guns in support.

The change left the 18th Division on the right flank next to the French. Linking with their 141 Regiment at Cemetery Copse above Hangard Cemetery, 6/Northants from 54 Brigade handed over 1,000 yards to 7/RW Kents of the 53rd, who had replaced 10/Essex in front of Lancer Wood. The Kents made way for 55 Brigade 1,300 yards further on at V.13.a.5.0. At 2,000 yards, its frontage was the longest and two battalions divided it between them, 8/East Surreys going to V.8.c.3.9 and 7/Buffs, who relieved the first occupants, 7/Queens, from there to V.2.d.7.3, 300 yards short of an embankment on the railway. The Buffs' headquarters in a mound on the southern side of a long cutting on it at V.1.b.1.7 was 1,350 yards east of Brigadier General Wood's in Monument Farm chateau, 'a handsome, two storied house in a walled rectangular yard, spacious stables and barns around the yard'. Wood found it 'thoroughly comfortable' and 'slept upstairs in a spacious bedroom every night'.[10]

As much of this line marked the limit of the Australian advance on 30 March, the 18th Division found when it began arriving next morning just 'a number of slits and organised shell holes connected in places to form a rough trench system, but there was no wire out'. The wet weather and intermittent German shelling made improvements difficult; in daylight they were impossible. At least the flat, open ground favoured the defenders, provided their crude shelters survived the bombardment before any assault. Repeating what many British commanders had said since March 21, Lee directed that: 'all positions

III Corps' dispositions around Villers-Bretonneux at dawn on 4 April 1918.

were to be "held to the last"'. If lost, immediate counterattacks were to retake them.[11]

These orders had a special ring for the Australians because 35 Battalion held the longest and most exposed part of the Fifth Army's line. Straddling the obvious axis of assault on Villers-Bretonneux, it stretched 2,800 yards southwest from 8/Rifle Brigade on the Roman Road at P.28.d.5.4 to link with 7/Buffs past the railway. Three companies garrisoned it, each broken up into five or six man posts hastily dug on arrival. Like Lee's men, they were unprotected by wire and cut off by day. But they had brought a section of four Vickers guns from 9 Machine Gun Company with them and also picked up abandoned Lewis guns on the move in. The thirty machine guns fielded, well above the battalion norm, partly compensated for the thin manning.

The other problem confronting Lieutenant Colonel Henry Goddard, 35 Battalion's commander, was that no buffer existed between his front line and Villers-Bretonneux, two and a half miles back. To gain the necessary depth, he ordered his reserve company, quartered in the town with another section of machine guns, to dig a support line one and a half miles behind the front line. It began on the road at P.26.c.5.3 and headed south past the roadside airfields and their derelict hangars to the bridge over the railway cutting at V.1.b.5.6, 200 yards from 7/Buffs' headquarters in the mound. The work pushed 35 Battalion to the brink and Lee let Rosenthal move 33 Battalion to the town on 2 April to help. Two of its companies would man the support line when it was finished.

Stuck in Gentelles and often out of touch owing to shell fire bringing down the telephone lines, Rosenthal put Goddard, a gentle forty-eight-year old who had commanded dangerous Quinn's Post in the last months at Gallipoli, in charge of the Australians in and around Villers-Bretonneux. Morshead shared his headquarters in today's Rue Driot, which is, appropriately enough, just a stone's throw from the ANZAC Museum. The tower of the town church nearby made an excellent vantage point. 'A dead man or two and a pool of blood just inside the door gave it a tragic aspect', Goddard recalled.[12]

Villers-Bretonneux from the Australian front line on the N29.

Villers-Bretonneux   Roman Road (N29)

Initially comprising all four battalions of 9 Brigade, the dedicated counterattack force was now down to 34 and 36 Battalions, both of which were in the Gentelles Line in the Bois l'Abbé. On 2 April, they were ordered to work on the Cachy Switch, the loop of the Gentelles Line that began at the village. The most important stretch lapped around the eastern edge of Cachy, from where it parallelled the road to Villers-Bretonneux past the southeastern corner of the Bois d'Aquenne. Manned by the 24th Division, 11/King's (the 14th Division's pioneers) and the two Australian battalions, the Gentelles/Aubigny Line itself was the main defensive barrier behind the town, though nowhere near complete. The Canadian Cavalry and 7 Cavalry Brigades from the 3rd Cavalry Division were in reserve around Boves, another four miles west, and the 2nd Cavalry Division was behind them near Amiens.

Lieutenant Colonel Henry Goddard.

Except for the Australian units, all of these formations, like those in the line, were tired. But at least XIX Corps was deployed in some depth and the field artillery of five divisions and the guns of five heavy brigades covered its front. As of 2 April, it no longer belonged to the Fifth Army but the Fourth, the name change reviving the title of the army Rawlinson had led on the Somme in 1916. Rawlinson himself had reverted from Fayolle's command to Haig's.

The Eve of the Attack
Taking advantage of better weather on 3 April, German aircraft buzzed the line east of Villers-Bretonneux. Hitherto spasmodic, German shelling increased, Lancer Wood, Gentelles, Cachy, the Bois l'Abbé and Villers-Bretonneux receiving particular attention. Night brought

Looking north from the southern end of the Australian support line towards the N29.

Vaire Wood   Roman Road (N29)   Hamel Wood

Villers-Bretonneux church. The towers were used as observation posts.

torrential rain. D Company, 33 Battalion left to deepen the support line and 6/Londons arrived exhausted from Amiens. They were to relieve 35 Battalion on the following night, allowing it to rejoin 34 and 36 Battalions in the counterattack role.

The signs of an imminent attack were confirmed when a prisoner captured by 7/Buffs at 3.45 am on 4 April said that it would come at dawn. Despite the rain and the pitch darkness, a great deal of movement was also detected around Marcelcave and Warfusée. Aiming to reach the line Gentelles Wood-Blangy-Tronville seven miles distant, five German divisions were preparing to assault the six-mile front the Fourth Army held south of the Somme. Alongside them, twelve more would strike the French First Army across the nine-mile front to Grivesnes. If the attack was successful, Ludendorff intended to push for Amiens next day. As heavy guns were now shelling the city, he had already achieved one objective.

NOTES

1. Nichols, op. cit., p. 303.
2. P. Simkins, 'The War Experience of a Typical Kitchener Division: The 18th Division, 1914-18' in H. Cecil and P. Liddle (eds), *Facing Armageddon* (Leo Cooper, 1996), p. 301.
3. J.M. Bourne, Essay on Brig. Gen. E.A. Wood, unpublished; Diary/Journal Account of R. Cude, 26 March 1918, CON/RC, Imperial War Museum (IWM).
4. Chell quoted in L. Macdonald, *To The Last Man* (Viking, 1998), p. 332.
5. Middlebrook, op. cit., p. 327; Haig, D, 29 March 1918, Haig Papers, Acc. 3155, National Library of Scotland.
6. P.J. Campbell, *The Ebb and Flow of Battle* (OUP, 1979), pp. 50-1; Cude D, 5 April 1918; Macdonald, op. cit., p. 181.
7. Macdonald, op. cit., p. 344; W. Smyth (17 Bn AIF), D, c. 5 April 1918, PR00927, AWM.
8. Nichols, op. cit., p. 306; Cude D, 31 March 1918.
9. *OH*, pp. 523-4; R. McMullin, *Pompey Elliott* (Scribe, 2002), p. 374.
10. 'Account of the Operations of 55 Infantry Brigade 1-6 April 1918', WO 95/2048, TNA; F.M. Cutlack, *The Australians: Their Final Campaign, 1918* (Sampson, Low & Marston, 1919), p.172; Nichols, op. cit., p. 306.
11. 'The 18th Division in the Defence of Amiens', 18 Div WD, April 1918, Item 21/A/1, AWM 45; Nichols, op. cit., p. 305.
12. Goddard quoted in D. Coombes, *Morshead* (OUP, 2001), p. 59.

Chapter Four

ATTACK AND COUNTERATTACK

At 5.15 am on 4 April, Villers-Bretonneux was smothered with high explosive and gas, costing 6/Londons, only 370 strong to begin with, over 100 more men. The front line and surrounding villages were also pummelled. From 6.15 am, the shelling concentrated on the forward area, where smoke from the bursting shells, the dawn drizzle and a heavy fog limited visibility to 100 yards. At 6.30 am, the wet and cold German infantry of XIV Corps north of the Roman Road and XI Corps south of it started out towards the equally miserable defenders.

The 14th (Light) Division
Knowing what the bombardment foreshadowed, General Skinner gave hasty orders at 6.50 am that led to 10/Hussars and 3/Dragoon Guards from 6 Cavalry Brigade deploying either side of 43 Brigade on Hill 104. But the information reaching his headquarters at Fouilloy was confused and out of date. The first reports of heavy shelling came in from 42 Brigade at 7.10 am and from 41 Brigade at 7.30 am. Skinner's 8.10 am message to 43 Brigade suggested there was little to worry about:

> *If we are attacked probably 41st Bde will get just the fringe of the attack which may come from the SE. There is a stout Brigade of Anzacs between us & MARCELCAVE. Enemy shelling on our front appears from here now to have been reduced considerably. We propose to send you some breakfast in a car as soon as we can.*

At 8.20 am a report arrived from 41 Brigade: 'so far as can be ascertained no infantry action has taken place.' Ten minutes later, 'The 42nd Inf Bde reported that enemy were in our line in P.22 (41st Bde. Front)'. Luck was not with the 14th Division. The relief it had just carried out was not completed until 4 am and, through a mix-up, the outgoing cavalry did not hand their machine guns over. Not only were the men very tired and lacking firepower but the attack started before they had seen in daylight the ground they were expected to hold.[1]

Delivering the main blow in XIV Corps' sector, the 228th Division fell on 41 Brigade. Shortly after the attack intensified at 7 am, 8/Rifle Brigade broke. The panic unnerved 7/Rifle Brigade and both battalions fell back 500 yards to a rough support line in front of the north-south

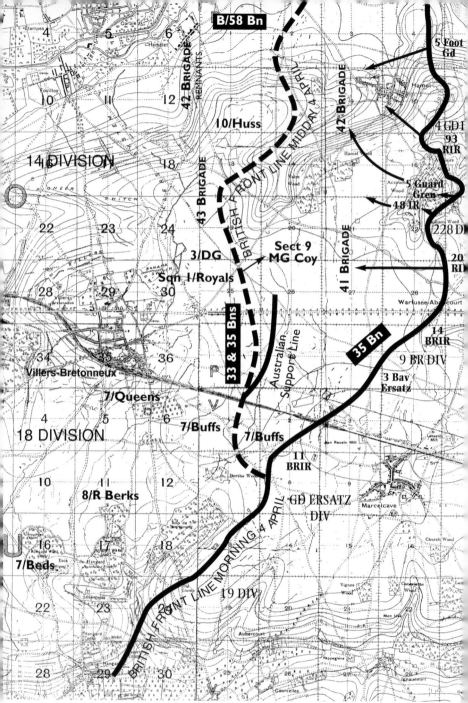

The situation around Villers-Bretonneux at midday on 4 April 1918.

road from Hamel. Conveniently located behind Accroche Wood, 8/King's Royal Rifle Corps (KRRC), 41 Brigade's third battalion, was ordered to hold this road from there to the Roman Road. Skinner also sent up three companies of 9/Scottish Rifles from 43 Brigade. The resulting rally was brief. In the 228th Division's next surge, 48 IR on the right tore ahead of 207 Reserve Infantry Regiment (RIR) on the Roman Road. 41 Brigade disintegrated, the rout continuing until the survivors reached the 43rd's line 3,000 yards rearwards at 10 am. Skinner did not know for certain what had happened until 11.25 am. Reports of 42 Brigade's collapse came in then as well.

Supported by British guns on the northern bank of the Somme, 42 Brigade had initially held firm. 'Everything still apparently normal on 42 Inf Bde front', the divisional message log recorded at 9.50 am. Shortly after, 'enemy have obtained footing on ridge [east of Hamel]'. But the real danger lay on the right flank, which 41 Brigade's flight had left hanging. Pouring through the breach on the coat-tails of 48 IR, 5 Guard Grenadiers from the 4th Guards Division turned northwest and crashed through Hamel and Vaire Woods and into 10/Hussars, which Skinner had sent forward to reconnoitre. A Squadron tried to parry the blow by seizing the eastern end of Hamel Wood but pulled back after losing fifty horses to machine gun fire.[2]

Realising that they might be cut off, 9/Rifle Brigade and 5/Ox and Bucks gave way as the rest of the 4th Guards came over the Wolfsberg. Another rout followed as the two battalions careered down the rear slope and through the depth battalion, 9/KRRC. Trying to stem the rot, Brigadier General George Forster remained at 42 Brigade's headquarters in Hamel, was captured at midday and killed by a stray bullet soon afterwards. His broken formation scuttled across the Somme flats past Bouzencourt and reached Vaire on the south bank at 11.45 am. There it encountered the Australians of B Company, 58 Battalion, which had crossed the river earlier to occupy some advanced posts straddling the exits on the southeastern edge of the village.

The collapse of 42 Brigade. The view is westward from the Wolfsberg.

Looking up at the northern slope of the spur that ran down from Hill 104 towards Hamel, the company commander, Captain Harold Ferres, saw that the Germans would be blocked if 42 Brigade took up a line across it. He made 'strenuous efforts' to rally them but 'the officers leading the retirement, when remonstrated with, protested that their orders were to fall back'. Conversely, parties from 10/Hussars that had become detached after their attack enthusiastically joined Ferres' men. At noon orders arrived from a furious Elliott in Corbie 'to stop all stragglers and compel them to fight'. Ferres collected about 500 and by 2.55 pm they had dug a line of posts that followed the road up the spur to link with the rest of 10/Hussars on 43 Brigade's left. On the river, the Australians edged towards Bouzencourt. Thanks largely to the artillery, which fired over open sights, the hastily improvised position stood.[3]

Convinced that the 14th Division was no longer fit to fight, Watts ordered the 3rd Cavalry Division at 5 pm to relieve it. Still relatively intact, 43 Brigade and 11/Kings stayed on in reserve while the rest of the division reformed in the Aubigny Line. Elliott had been warned in the morning that 15 Brigade would be crossing the Somme during the afternoon to strengthen the Fourth Army's left flank. At 12.15 am on 5 April, 58, 59 and 60 Battalions in that order held a 4,000 yard frontage that stretched from Vaire to P.14.c.3.0 on the Fouilloy-Warfusée Road opposite Vaire Wood, where 6 Cavalry Brigade took charge. 57 Battalion at Hamelet augmented the reserve behind them.

9 Brigade

From his headquarters in what is now Marcelcave Buttes National Cemetery, Major Henry Carr saw that the opening bombardment had missed A Company, in the centre of 35 Battalion's line, altogether. At 6.30 am the mist briefly cleared to reveal platoons from the 9th Bavarian Reserve (BR) Division's three regiments, 14 BRIR, 3 Bavarian Ersatz IR and 11 BRIR, assembling on the western outskirts of Warfusée and Marcelcave and along the D42 between them, up

Marcelcave Buttes National Cemetery, headquarters of A Company, 35 Battalion.

which the 61st Division had attacked a week before. B Company and A Company on its left shot them down, not once but three times.

On the right, the railway embankment bisected C Company's line at V.3.c.2.9, masking the posts on one side from those on the other. Captain Gilbert Coghill, the company commander, was finishing a chicken and champagne breakfast when the light of a burning house showed 11 BRIR to be deploying from Marcelcave. Passing the order to open up only on his signal, he leapt onto the embankment where every post could see him. When the Germans were forty yards away, Coghill raised his arm. He was instantly shot through the arm, but the Germans were obliterated by the fire going the other way.

At 7 am these disjointed attacks fizzled out and the entire German line advanced. 35 Battalion's War Diary graphically recorded what happened next:

> Our SOS was sent up and was immediately responded to by an accurate barrage which fell on the dense masses of advancing infantry, cutting gaps in his formations. In addition to artillery fire, the enemy was subjected to the maximum firepower of all units in the line – causing him very large losses.

Then 8/Rifle Brigade across the Roman Road folded and B Company was outflanked. Parts of 14 BRIR struck its rear or headed for the roadside airfields. B Company withdrew to the empty support line but the Germans were there as well. Unable to break clear, it continued westwards covered by the section from 9 Machine Gun Company. Two of the section's four guns were lost.[4]

Major Carr initially thought that the men flowing back on his left were German prisoners. On seeing that they were B Company and the Germans intermingled, he informed Coghill and tried to form a defensive flank but B Company's withdrawal went past it, forcing Carr to pull his own company back in conformity. It halted south of the airfield hangars with its left 200 yards north of the crossroads in P.31.c. B Company had finally regrouped at the western end of the airfields, which was close to P.25.c.1.3, the Hamel/Roman Road junction about 700 yards from the town and the site of a roundabout on the N29 today.

Carr's message had struck Coghill like a thunderbolt. 7/Buffs on his right had already pulled out and he was propping up that flank with nothing more than a Lewis gun and the optimistic hope that 11 BRIR had had enough. But the Germans soon reached the cemetery where Carr's headquarters had been and enfiladed his left. Isolated and with both flanks open, Coghill ordered a withdrawal to the support line. The platoons covered each other as C Company fell back and gained touch

**The view from the end of the Australian support line towards the front
line, from which 35 Battalion withdrew.**

with 7/Buffs near the railway bridge at V.1.b.5.6, where the Australian
support line ended. Wounded again during the withdrawal, Coghill was
patched up at the aid post 35 Battalion had set up under it.

Meanwhile, Goddard was dispersing 33 Battalion from Villers-
Bretonneux to the support line. D Company, which had only just
returned from working on it during the night, and A Company came
across Carr's line after 1,200 yards. By 7.45 am, with D Company next
to Carr's men and A Company alongside Coghill's, they had filled the
gap between them. B Company went up half an hour later and Carr
used it to extend his left towards the hangars. As B Company was down
to sixty-one men after suffering the heaviest casualties at Lancer Wood,
that flank still remained very weak. Goddard reinforced it with C
Company, 33 Battalion's strongest, with 149 men under Captain Walter
Duncan.

Leaving at 9 am, the four platoons hurried along the Roman Road
to the junction, where Duncan deployed them from B Company's left
to P.25.c.4.7 on the Hamel road, 250 yards inside the 14th Division's
sector. One of 9 Machine Gun Company's two remaining sections,
which Rosenthal had despatched at 7 am, took up a position 900 yards
further along the road. Together with Duncan's company, it checked
207 IR as it followed up 41 Brigade. At 10.15 am, a squadron of
1/Royal Dragoons, 6 Cavalry Brigade's reserve regiment, fortuitously
arrived to plug the gap between Duncan's flank and 3/Dragoon Guards
on Hill 104. As the cavalry had brought with them three Vickers guns
and a Hotchkiss, the fire against the Germans became torrential and
they fell back towards Warfusée.

Goddard now sought more room on the Roman Road and at 10.27
am ordered B and D Companies of 33 Battalion astride it to drive 800
yards eastwards to P.25.d.8.3, just beyond the airfields. Joined by
1/Royal Dragoons, the advance started well but 228 IR rallied and
counterattacked with 14 BRIR at 11.15 am. Duncan's men got the
upper hand after a sharp fight around the airfield huts and were on
their objective at 11.35 am. On the left, the cavalry closed up to the
machine gun section that had been isolated on the Hamel road for three
hours.

The Australian line was now everywhere in touch and tied in on both flanks. As the other machine gun section sent up by Rosenthal had joined the two guns that survived the withdrawal, it bristled with ten Vickers guns altogether. Clogged with mud – in many cases so badly as to be almost unserviceable – rifles and Lewis guns were quickly cleaned. 6/Londons generously exchanged six of 35 Battalion's dirty Lewis guns for six of their clean ones, a gesture, says the 35th's War Diary, that was 'of considerable help'.[5]

As the battle was subsiding, General Watts had directed Rosenthal to move 34 and 36 Battalions northwest and southwest of Villers-Bretonneux so that one of them could block another breakthrough no matter where it came. Rosenthal convinced him that counterattacks would be easier to control if the two battalions were put under Goddard in assembly areas close to the town. Shortly after 1 pm, 36 Battalion had deployed in the hollow on the southern side of it, where A and B Companies at the head of the hollow were just 500 yards from the orchard behind Monument Farm. Lieutenant Colonel John Milne, the battalion commander, remained at Goddard's headquarters for instant briefing if a counterattack were needed. Occupying the bigger hollow on the northern side of Villers-Bretonneux, 34 Battalion looked across at the spur on which the Australian National Memorial now stands.

The 18th Division
At 6 am a rain of shells ended General Wood's restful stay at Monument Farm. He was unhurt and 7/Queens, in reserve behind it, got off lightly but the telephone links to the front line were cut. Heavy firing was heard around 6.30 am. Unable to push C Company, 35 Battalion off the railway, 11 BRIR had shifted its axis of attack

Looking east along the Roman Road from Villers-Bretonneux towards the airfield huts and hangars, the scene of sharp fighting on 4 April.

Hangars

Roman Road

southwards against 7/Buffs, who held at first but then left their positions, probably realising that the Germans would try again. Struck earlier by how worn they looked, Captain Coghill floundered 500 yards through the mud to find the closest company commander, Lieutenant D.G. Ferguson, who readily agreed when Coghill asked him whether his men would return if C Company's Lewis guns covered them. Saying 'We'll stand by you, Anzacs', the men seemed willing and reoccupied the line, only to retire again.[6]

Ferguson's company had gone back to the railway bridge at V.1.b.5.6, where C Company joined them an hour later. When Wood found out, he secured 55 Brigade's left flank by sending Lieutenant Colonel A.L. Ransome, the Buffs' commander, a company from 7/Queen's with instructions to string it along the railway. Two more Queen's companies were readied on the D23 in case the Germans broke through. But the losses inflicted by the British barrage made them pause and at 10.30 am they saturated the area with gas instead. Not taking any chances, Wood further reinforced the Buffs with a company of 6/Londons from Villers-Bretonneux. Lee had given him the battalion at 8.30 am.[7]

The right flank of 7/Buffs was still firmly linked to 8/E. Surreys, which reported its line intact at 11 am. As 55 Brigade's War Diary explained, the Guards Ersatz Division's attack was lighter and 'directed rather across their front at the battalion on their right than at them'. Holding 53 Brigade's line, that battalion was 7/RW Kents. Its War Diary comments: 'At 6.30 am enemy attacked left front coy at about V.13.central but was driven back to his trenches by L.G. and rifle fire'. A second attempt was barely noticed. Above Hangard, the British guns subdued the German, and the 19th Division's attack against 6/Northants and the French hardly got going. At 10 am Brigadier Generals Higginson and Sadleir-Jackson ordered their reserve battalions in Gentelles to move up in support, 8/R. Berks to the northern end of Hangard Wood East and 7/Bedfords behind the Cachy-Hangard road below Hangard Wood West.[8]

The Attack Renewed

As success in the offensive phase of war depends above all else on maintaining momentum, another drive might have been expected north of the Roman Road, where the greatest gain had been made and the new line was very fragile. The splendidly named commander of the 4th Guards Division, Major General Count von Finckenstein, urged this course but was overruled because the only formation that could have undertaken it had to be retained as a reserve and the British artillery across the Somme held XIV Corps in enfilade. Instead, the Germans elected to renew the attack on XI Corps' front south of the Roman Road with the lightly used 19th Division striking the right of the 18th Division, and the French in Hangard, at 4 pm, and the 9th BR and Guards Ersatz Divisions chiming in half an hour later.

The defenders realised as the afternoon wore on that the next attack would come from the southeast. They picked up a lot of movement east of Lancer Wood and the German artillery was concentrating on the line south of the railway. At 3 pm it fired a hurricane bombardment heavily flavoured with gas. Skirmishers advanced from the line of the Marcelcave-Démuin road at 4 pm. The 19th Division's assault had begun.

Smashed by the bombardment, 6/Northants initially back-pedalled 1,500 yards to the Bedfords' position near the Cachy-Hangard road, which also started to waver until steadied by Sadleir-Jackson, who galloped back and forth abusing his men. The Northants then gained touch with 141 Regiment at Hangard Copse on Hill 99, the spur above Hangard. Clinging to the western edge of the village, the French had lost Hangard Cemetery and Cemetery Copse, though they recaptured them later. On the right of the attack, 8/E. Surreys folded after mud jammed many weapons and casualties became severe. They went back 3,000 yards to the Villers-Bretonneux-Hangard road. Only eighty men reached it. The Surreys' withdrawal left Lancer Wood north of V.13.a.5.0 – over half its area – entirely open. At 5 pm the Germans belted through and 7/RW Kents narrowly escaped being cut off. Passing through Hangard Wood East they reformed on the road 1,000 yards south of the Surreys.

At the northern end of the wood, 8/R. Berks had no idea what had happened until they saw the Germans moving towards their left flank. Watching from his headquarters behind a pile of mangelwurzels, Lieutenant Colonel Robert Dewing yelled 'Fire' when they were 200 yards away. As the volley tore into it, the advance shuddered. Seizing the moment, Dewing called for a bayonet charge but was wounded leading it out. His batman, Private F. Bailey, was carrying him back when a stray bullet went through Dewing's mouth, killing him instantly. Bailey was hit too but the tin of bully beef in his haversack saved him. Although Dewing's bold action blunted the attack, it left the Berks very exposed. At 6 pm they withdrew to the Villers-Bretonneux-Hangard road as well, linking up with 8/E. Surreys but remaining out of touch with 7/RW Kents on the right. Fifty-eight men got back. The

Germans now held Hangard Wood East.

The 9th BR Division's assault, which directly threatened Villers-Bretonneux, was even more dramatic. Anticipating a retirement when 8/Surreys' collapse unmasked his right flank, Lieutenant Colonel Ransome told the company of 6/Londons attached to 7/Buffs to form a support line by extending 1,000 yards southwest from his headquarters at the railway mound. When 3 Bavarian Ersatz IR advanced astride the tracks with 11 BRIR to its south at 4.30 pm, the Londons covered the hasty withdrawal of the Buffs towards Monument Farm, where Wood was trying to impose order on chaos.[9]

At 4 pm, an observer on the top floor of Wood's headquarters had seen the 19th Division swarm across the plateau to the southeast and the British line fall back before it. Gas drenched the main building at that moment, flooring Private Cude:

> *It is extraordinary in its intensity . . . I have never felt his gas before but this time I catch it pretty hot. Looking back on it, I wonder how I survived. I was on the ground writhing in agony, and was quite prepared for the finish, when suddenly, we get the order to move off at once and to our consternation, we find that the Boys are retiring fast, and even as we leave the back door, Jerry is coming in at the front. Then follows a wild chase through the grounds, and I am blown sky high by a shell that dropped just underneath me, and for a period which seemed hours, I was buried.[10]*

Wood was outside readying the companies of 7/Queen's at the farm to counterattack when a flurry of shells slammed into the orchard and ignited some of the outbuildings just as the first stragglers arrived from the line. Panic-stricken, many of the Queen's joined them as they burst through 36 Battalion in the hollow further back, 'reporting that the enemy were advancing in thousands'. Wood eventually managed to assemble about 180 men from 7/Queen's a few hundred yards behind the orchard and the Buffs were rallied near Villers-Bretonneux station. But the Australian line had also gone.

When the Buffs hurtled rearwards, the right of C Company, 35 Battalion bent back to form a defensive flank. Those in the adjacent posts thought a withdrawal was underway and started back themselves. The movement rippled along the line 33 and 35 Battalions held between them until only B and C Companies of the 33rd under Captain Duncan were still in place astride the Roman Road.

'You Must Counterattack at Once'

News of the British retirement had reached Goddard in the town at about 4.45 pm. Confident the cavalry would guarantee his left flank, he decided to shift 34 Battalion from the counterattack position behind them to a blocking line behind the threatened right flank. Goddard had no sooner given the order than word arrived that his right was coming back in disarray. Simultaneously, Carr dashed in yelling that 'the whole line had retired' and that Goddard's headquarters was now the most advanced position. Rushing outside to see for himself, Lieutenant Colonel Morshead met one of his own officers, who confirmed the report. Morshead directed him to post Lewis guns on all the roads into the town. In addition, six armoured cars and five Canadian motor machine gun batteries, sent up by Rawlinson, had come into action on the outskirts at 4 pm.

The closest intact unit to the breakthrough was 36 Battalion. Giving the railway as the axis, Goddard told its commander, 'Colonel, you must counter-attack at once'. Lieutenant Colonel Milne, a former private in the prewar British Army, saluted and left. Though the three battered companies of 6/Londons still in the town were no longer under Goddard's command, they willingly agreed to support the attack. His staff officer, Captain Hugh Connell, went to the railway bridge on the D23 at the southeastern corner of Villers-Bretonneux to reorganise stragglers. Lastly, Goddard instructed Morshead to locate 34 Battalion, cancel its rearward move, and have it counterattack from the north of the town.[11]

Restoring the Line
Racing back to his headquarters in U.5.a, 'a slight excavation on the roadside on the Villers-Bretonneux-Hangard road covered with a tarpaulin', Milne saw that the weight of the assault was south of the railway and opted to counterattack on that side rather than astride the track as Goddard had directed. 'Company commanders to assemble at the double' he shouted breathlessly. The battalion was already in assault formation so his orders were brief:

The enemy has broken through on our

An elderly resident of Villers-Bretonneux who remained alone in her house throughout the fighting on 4 April.

immediate front and we must counterattack at once. Bushelle, your company will be on the left. Rodd, B Company will be in the centre. Tedder, C Company will take the right, and I shall send immediately to the CO of the Queen's and ask him to co-operate. Bushelle, your left flank will rest on the railway embankment. The 35th are on the other side. Attack in one wave. D Company, under Captain Gadd, I shall hold you in reserve here in the sunken road. Get ready. There's no time to waste.

'How far shall we go', asked Captain John Bushelle of A Company. Milne's answer was simple: 'Go till you're stopped and hold on at all costs'.

Milne had seen a 'stoutly built figure, with overcoat and walking stick', whom he thought was the 'CO of the Queen's'. It turned out to be Brigadier General Wood. He was reforming his men behind the orchard when Milne's adjutant turned up with 'a cordial invitation' to co-operate on C Company's right flank. Wood immediately accepted and said he would personally lead this part of the attack. As the Australians shook out on their start line, Milne walked along it, turned and said: 'Good-bye, boys. It's neck or nothing'.[12]

At 5.15 pm, the line went forward at a brisk jog and crested the lip of the hollow just as waves of 3 Bavarian Ersatz IR were emerging from the orchard. The Bavarians recoiled but recovered swiftly. A crunching fusillade erupted from the orchard's edge and the hedges and damaged buildings of the farm, which gave excellent cover. A machine gun also opened from the shelter of a haystack a little north of it. B Company in the centre was hardest hit and C Company and the Queen's on its right also lost heavily. A Company, furthest away on the left, was the least bothered but stalled nonetheless. The assault diverged.

B Company moved towards the northern side of the orchard but the fire from there and from the haystack held it up, and badly wounded its commander, Major Brent Rodd. Captain Bushelle got both companies moving again by having them hug the railway. Finding themselves outflanked, the Germans in the orchard, the farm and, once the advance crossed the D23, in Monument Wood, started withdrawing. Some machine guns on the mound by the railway cutting between 7/Buffs' old headquarters and the bridge at the end of the Australian support line brought A Company to a halt at V.1.b.3.6. Enfiladed by a machine gun concealed among haystacks at U.12.b.6.8, B Company was forced to ground after swinging around the wood and remained behind A Company's right. Between them, the two companies had advanced

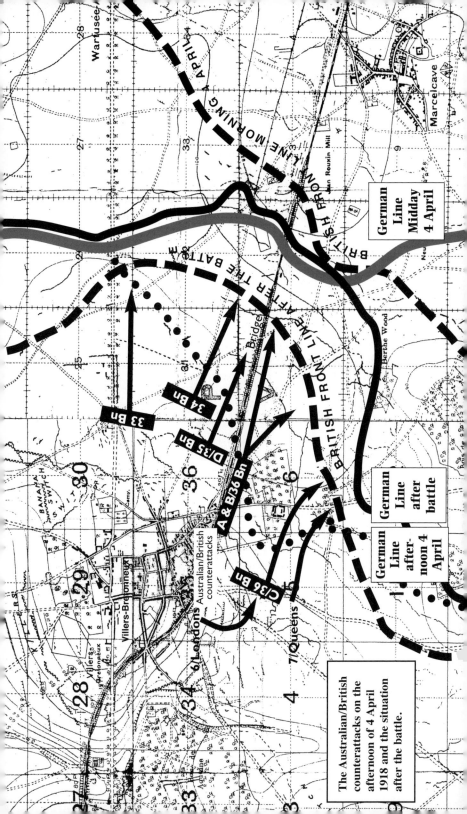

The Australian/British counterattacks on the afternoon of 4 April 1918 and the situation after the battle.

A 1918 view of the mound where the Australian counterattack was halted on the afternoon of 4 April. It was taken in a second attack that night.

The mound today. Note the railway bridge, which was where the Australian support line ended.

Bridge

1,500 yards.

C Company had crabbed towards the southern side of the orchard. As it approached, some Germans, shielded by the poplars that lined the D23 south of the farm in 1918, scarpered 400 yards to the crossroads at U.6.c.5.3, the site of Crucifix Corner Cemetery today, and set up a machine gun that halted progress. Blown up earlier in the Bois l'Abbé and sniped once, Second Lieutenant Albert Amess, the only officer left in C Company, urged on the Queen's, who were stuck behind its right rear. Three runners died and Amess was sniped again before his message got through and the advance restarted. As the Germans were abandoning the farm and wood on account of Bushelle's dash to the north, the fire from that flank slackened but the crossroads' machine gun was not affected and it kept the Queen's off the D23. Even Wood could do nothing. Only when Amess, hit once more, led C Company across did the gunners flee. It dug in facing south with its right on the

D23 at U.6.c.5.8, half a mile past its start point.

Monument Farm and Wood had been regained but the new line was almost a mile long. Caused by a divergent advance that cost the three assault companies 150 men, a quarter of 36 Battalion's strength, the gaps in it were huge. With night falling, Milne filled them with his reserve, D Company, and the three companies of 6/Londons that had come down from Villers-Bretonneux and followed after the assault. Though Milne now had what he termed 'a good solid line', there was nothing behind it. He also thought the Germans might have already tried subterfuge in front of it:

2/Lieutenant Albert Amess.

At 6.30 pm ... a man dressed as a British officer came to our lines in the vicinity of U.6.d.9.7 (held by B Company) and ordered the men to retire, which they refused to do. He was wearing an Officer's tunic, a private's cap with a Queen's badge and the name G.E. MARTIN written inside. He carried a pack (containing some fancy work) instead of fighting order, which aroused suspicion. He was closely questioned and asked to produce his papers. This he failed to do, and in addition, he could give no satisfactory explanation of his conduct and presence. He was shot.

Whether the man was German or not – Bean thought he probably was not – the chances of 36 Battalion taking him prisoner at such a critical time were poor. In this regard, Milne's after-action report implied a lot more than it said: 'Owing to the rapidity of our counter attack and the intensity of enemy fire, it was impossible to bother about prisoners, only three being sent back'.[13]

While Milne had been getting the counterattack underway, Captain Connell and Captain Raleigh Sayers, who commanded D Company, 35 Battalion, ran to the railway bridge on the D23. Finding no-one from the rest of the battalion to rally but seeing 14 BRIR half a mile ahead and 3 Bavarian Ersatz IR nearing Monument Farm, Connell helped Sayers form his men up immediately north of the tracks for a charge. As the Australians closed, the Germans broke. Sayers tackled three in

Monument Farm

7/Queens

C/36 Bn

D23

Villers-Bretonneux church

D/35 Bn (far side of railway)

B/36 Bn

A/36 Bn

The Australian counterattack on 4 April.

a shell hole. Unarmed because he had left his revolver at Goddard's headquarters, he brained one with the man's steel helmet and strangled the second; the third bolted. More Germans fled on seeing 36 Battalion advance on the other side of the railway. The machine guns on the mound eventually stopped the charge opposite Bushelle's left across the cutting.

When he heard that the Australians had withdrawn, Brigadier General Archie Seymour, the commander of 6 Cavalry Brigade, worried that the Germans would by-pass his line north of the Roman Road. As all his regiments were already holding it, he turned to 7 Cavalry Brigade, which had rushed up from Boves, and ordered 17/Lancers under Lieutenant Colonel T.P. Melvill to reconnoitre and form a defensive flank if necessary. When Melville galloped over Hill 104,

> *An amazing sight then burst into view. There were Australians as far as the eye could see, retiring in perfect order as on an Aldershot field day, with our dismounted cavalry doing likewise ... I could see no signs of the enemy, nor any apparent reason for the retirement.*

These were the companies of 33 Battalion that stayed on the Roman Road after the line on their right had gone. 14 BRIR was coming towards them and Sayers' counterattack had not yet begun. To avoid being cut off, they moved slowly back, intending to take up a new line closer to Villers-Bretonneux. Everything became clear to Melvill when he got closer: 'Once more I was dumbfounded. It looked as if the whole German army was advancing unmolested in extended order across the plain'.

The cavalry's arrival was a tonic for the Australians: 'Seeing them gallop into action with swords and lances drawn and moving quickly to where help was most needed enthused our men tremendously', Morshead wrote. Their response thrilled Melvill: 'As the retiring troops saw us pass through them, the whole line appeared to halt, as if with surprise at what they saw, then mechanically turn about and advance. It was a wonderful moment'. Dismounting, the cavalry opened up with their Hotchkisses, the Australians joined in and three armoured cars barrelled up the Roman Road with Vickers guns blazing to lend a hand. 14 BRIR wilted under the storm of fire and the Lancers extended southwards to link up with Sayers.

Morshead, meanwhile, had brought 34 Battalion around to the eastern outskirts of the town. Screened by the cavalry, it headed southeast at 6.20 pm to occupy the 800-yard stretch from the railway to P.31.a.8.2, whereupon 33 Battalion filled in from there to P.25.d.2.3 on the Roman Road and the cavalry took over north of it. The Australian line was now continuous but overlooked by the mound strongpoint.

In Villers-Bretonneux, Goddard was considering whether to advance to the old support line. The battalion commanders wondered whether their men would be too tired but Goddard thought the Germans were just as tired and likely to be caught napping. He gave the toughest task, the clearing of the mound and the bridge ahead of it, to the freshest battalion, the 34th, and dispensed with a preliminary barrage to ensure surprise. Arriving at 11 pm, Rosenthal concurred. Finally allowed to leave Gentelles, he had gone first to Sayers' location, where the mound was outlined against the night sky. The assault went in at 1 am.

When the first shots rang out, 34 Battalion's Lewis gunners hosepiped from the hip to keep the firers' heads down. Advancing south of the railway, where Bushelle had made room for it, D Company quickly overran the mound and the bridge before propping 150 yards further on. C Company had a harder fight on the other side, temporarily losing touch with 33 Battalion in the darkness as more and more men were drawn in. The 33rd itself had a sharp clash near the airfields but 36 Battalion and 17/Lancers met little opposition while conforming on the flanks. By 2.30 am, the Australians were back in their support position.[14]

The 18th Division patched up the front to the south. At 6.30 pm Lee ordered 11/Royal Fusiliers, in reserve at Gentelles, to re-establish the centre of his line by counterattacking past the northern tip of Hangard Wood East. Approaching the Villers-Bretonneux-Hangard road, the Fusiliers saw that 8/R. Berks were very thinly spread with a big gap on their right. As night was falling, they reinforced the Berks instead. In turn, 10/Essex moved up on the Fusiliers' right and gained touch with 7/RW Kents, whom they relieved. Further north, 8/E. Surreys edged forward to meet 7/Queen's 600 yards southwest of Monument Farm. 36 Battalion and 6/Londons relieved both battalions early next morning.

Though Villers-Bretonneux was saved, the Germans had come within a whisker of taking it. They had also advanced two miles against the French First Army, grabbing Moreuil, Rifle and Little Woods, all soaked in cavalry blood, and part of the Bois de Sénécat, from the eastern edge of which Amiens was visible, before strengthening resistance and logistics difficulties stopped them going further. Only the Somme front still offered some prospect of success, and Ludendorff ordered the attack to continue astride the river. Even if Amiens were not reached, the Allies might be deterred from sending troops to Flanders to counter the imminent *Georgette* offensive.

The Day After
When dawn broke on 5 April, the weather had cleared and 36 Battalion saw German formations emerge from Lancer Wood, march across its front at 800 yards' distance and extend from the railway as if to attack. 'These provided splendid targets for L.G. and rifle fire and great quantities of S.A.A. were despatched to the enemy with observed good results. His stretcher-bearers were active throughout the day', noted the Battalion War Diary. Covered by their artillery, the Germans dug in. North of the railway, 33 and 34 Battalions also saw a great deal of movement and were strongly shelled but no attack came.

North of the Roman Road at 11 am, 6 Cavalry Brigade, 15 Brigade and the British artillery on Hill 104 shredded 48 IR as it crested the Vaire Wood-Hamel spur half a mile away. Trying next, 35 Fusilier, the 228th Division's reserve regiment, got 150 yards before a hail of machine gun fire shattered it. A third attempt did not even get that far. The attack was called off. At 2 pm, Corporal Douglas Sayers of 58 Battalion, whose four-man post protected a machine gun several hundred yards east of Vaire, saw thirty Germans creeping along the Somme flats towards the village. Two of Sayers' men opened fire while he and the fourth man crawled behind them and shot seven. The rest fled when the Australians charged.

At 4 pm on the Luce flank, 6/Northants and the French lost Hangard Copse and the cemetery. Counterattacking at 7.20 pm, the Northants were illuminated by the light of a burning haystack and struck by machine gun fire that stopped them fifty yards from the Villers-Bretonneux road. Though wounded, their commander, Lieutenant Colonel Turner, urged them onward and they reached the road, retaking Hangard Copse. Shielded by Hill 99, the French regained the cemetery.

The day after. A street in Villers-Bretonneux on 5 April.

German attacks north of the Somme also went unrewarded. Ludendorff admitted that evening:

> *The battle was over by the 4th of April. The enemy's resistance was beyond our powers... In agreement with the commanders concerned, O.H.L.* [High Command] *was forced to take the extremely hard decision to abandon the attack on Amiens for good.*

Smaller attacks might be made, however, to support *Georgette* and if the local situation demanded it.[15]

The Absolute Limit

The battle reinforced Australian impressions that British troops were second-rate. Captain William Braithwaite thought 'Some English divisions are as good fighters as the Chinese Labour Corps'. Writing to his wife on the evening of 4 April, Major General John Monash, to whose 3rd Division 9 Brigade belonged, specifically criticised the 14th Division:

> *A new British Division came into the line, on my right flank, South of the Somme last night, and was this morning biffed out, making a bad break in the line, and exposing my right flank . . . Some of these Tommy Divisions are the absolute limit, and not worth the money it costs to put them into uniform. However, – I mustn't let myself go – you can doubtless read between the lines of all I have written in the recent past – bad troops, bad staffs, bad commanders.*[16]

Though there were mitigating arguments for the 14th Division, it had held the strongest part of the line, where even Carey's scratch force had

Major General John Monash.

done well. Moreover, its toughest critics were not the Australians but the British cavalry, one of whose officers wrote: 'The 14th Div were tired before they went in, but having once got into the line, they should have stayed there'. When the division wanted barbed wire afterwards for its sector of the Aubigny Line, Major General A. Harman, the commander of the 3rd Cavalry Division, scathingly asked whether 'it was proposed to put the wire in front or behind them, as judging by their performance he thought it was advisable to have something put behind them to keep them in their place'. Rawlinson thought the 14th 'did badly'.[17]

With the exception of 7/Buffs, who were shaky throughout, the same criticism could not be levelled at the British gunners, who helped retain Hill 104, and the 18th Division. 8/R. Berks and 6/Northants counterattacked vigorously, and Rosenthal lauded the spirit and determination in the decisive counterattack of 7/Queen's, as well as 6/Londons from the 58th Division. He reserved the greatest praise for the cavalry, a sentiment that was widely shared. 'No men could have done more than these cavalry did', Captain Ferres remarked. Morshead regarded them as the 'true British soldiers'.[18]

What about the Australians themselves? 35 Battalion had held a line one and a half times as long as the longest of the British brigade fronts and did so for five nights, longer than any of the British battalions had been in theirs. It went back only when the flanking units had gone. Badly understrength after its costly counterattack on Lancer Wood, 33 Battalion was the mainstay of the Australian left throughout the day, while 36 Battalion's counterattack, which turned the tide, and 34 Battalion's night counterattack, were both made at short notice over ground neither battalion had seen before.

The British paid due tribute. That arch-Australophobe, Private Cude, thought 36 Battalion's effort was 'simply wonderful'. Reflecting the mutual admiration between the cavalry and the Australians, Harman told Elliott that his men 'were very proud to have the opportunity of fighting alongside your splendid fellows' and looked forward to doing so again. Appropriately enough, Bean gave the credit for saving Villers-Bretonneux jointly to 9 Brigade and the 3rd Cavalry Division. Rawlinson said they had both fought magnificently.[19]

More Australian formations were arriving. As the attack developed on April 4, GHQ had given Rawlinson 5 Brigade, the first of the 2nd Division's brigades to reach the Somme from Flanders, and allotted the rest of the 5th Division to the Fourth Army. Rawlinson was delighted:

> I feel happier about the general situation, and I have now three brigades of Australians in reserve, so I think we shall be able to keep the Boche out of Amiens. I am to take over the Australian Corps on the 8th, with a front up to Albert. Hurrah![20]

By the morning of 6 April, 5 Brigade, commanded by Brigadier General Robert Smith, had relieved the 18th Division and 9 Brigade between the Roman Road and the French at Hangard. Still in charge of the sector, General Lee gave 7/RW Kents and 10/Essex to Smith for counterattacks. Headquartered at Bussy-les-Daours, three and a half miles west of Corbie, the 5th Division assumed responsibility from Villers-Bretonneux to the Somme. Its commander, Major General Talbot Hobbs, sent 14 Brigade to relieve 6 Cavalry Brigade on Hill 104 next to 15 Brigade, and 8 Brigade replaced the 24th Division in reserve in the Gentelles Line. Australian units now held the entire front line but they were under the control of General Butler and III Corps. Worn out after ably fighting a difficult defensive battle for over a fortnight, Watts had handed over to him at Dury at 8 pm the night before.

NOTES

1. In/Out Messages, 3-5 April 1918, 14 Div WD, Item 21/89, AWM 45.
2. 10/Hussars WD, 4 April 1918, WO 95/1153, TNA.
3. 58 Bn WD, 4 April 1918, Item 23/75, Roll 96, AWM 4.
4. 35 Bn WD, 4 April 1918, Item 23/52, Roll 71, AWM 4; H.A. Goddard, 'Villers-Bretonneux Mar 30 – Apr 6 1918', undated account, 3DRL 2379, AWM.
5. 'Report on Defensive Operations East of Villers-Bretonneux, Apr 4-5 1918' dated 6 April 1918, 33 Bn WD, Item 23/50, Roll 69, AWM 4.
6. *OH*, pp. 319-20.
7. 7/Buffs WD, 4 April 1918, WO 95/2049, TNA.
8. 'Account of 55 Bde Operations, 1-6 April 1918', 55 Bde WD, April 1918, WO 95/2048, TNA; 7/RW Kents WD, 4 April 1918, WO 95/2040, TNA.
9. 6 Northants WD, 4 April 1918, WO 95/2044, TNA; 8/R. Berks WD, 4 April 1918, WO 95/2037, TNA; Nichols, op. cit., pp. 313-3; 55 Bde Account.
10. Cude, D, 5 April 1918.
11. 33 Bn Report; 35 Bn WD, 4 April 1918; *OH*, p. 337.
12. RSM A.R. Horwood (36 Bn) quoted in *OH*, p. 340.
13. 'Report on 36 Bn Operations 4-6 April 1918', and Out Messages 4-6 April, 1918, 36 Bn WD, Item 25/3, Roll 72, AWM 4; *OH*, pp. 344-5.
14. *OH*, pp. 346-7; Report dated 6 April 1918, 34 Bn WD, Item 23/51, Roll 70, AWM; J. Edwards, *Never A Backward Step. A History of the First 33rd Battalion AIF* (Bettong Books, 1996), pp. 76-7.
15. 36 Bn WD, 5 April 1918; 54 Bde WD, 5 April 1918, WO 95/2042, TNA; Ludendorff in *Military Operations II*, p. 137.
16. Braithwaite to mother, 7 April 1918, PR00349, AWM; Monash to wife, 4 April 1918, Monash Collection, 3DRL/2316, AWM.
17. A. Home, *The Diary of a World War 1 Cavalry Officer* (Costello, 1985), p. 166; Elliott and Rawlinson quoted in McMullin, op. cit., pp. 375, 433.
18. 9 Bde Report, Rosenthal to Harman, both 7 April 1918, 9 Bde WD, Item 23/9, Roll 18, AWM 4; 58 Bn WD, 4 April 1918; 33 Bn Report.
19. Cude D, 5 April 1918; McMullin, op. cit., p. 377.
20. F.B. Maurice, *The Life of General Lord Rawlinson of Trent* (Cassell, 1928), p. 216.

Chapter Five

HANGARD AND AFTER

Notwithstanding the Australian presence, the Fourth Army's tactical position with regard to Amiens had deteriorated. With its apex at the Bois de Sénécat lying six miles southwest of Hangard, the salient the Germans had driven into the French line south of the Luce was well behind Rawlinson's right. This offered them a northwesterly advance past Gentelles and Cachy that would outflank Villers-Bretonneux on its way to the Roman Road and thence Amiens. Their gains either side of the Roman Road brought their guns a mile closer to the city. Rawlinson and Haig represented the danger to Foch.

For his part, Foch had already appreciated the need for action. His General Directive No. 2 of 3 April sought to free Amiens by driving the Germans 'farther away' from it. Their attack next day expedited matters. Foch decreed a joint Anglo-French offensive to regain the line Moreuil-Démuin-Aubercourt-Warfusée, roughly the front held on 28 March between the Avre and the Somme. Two preliminary operations were to go ahead immediately, one by the French First Army to clear part of the west bank of the Avre, the other by the Fourth Army 'to clean up the woods and ravine north and north-east of Hangard'. Reflecting the urgency, 5 Brigade had received its orders to take over the line south of the Roman Road, from which the cleanup would start, at 7 pm on 5 April. Those for the cleanup itself arrived half an hour later. They stated that it must be done by 7 April at the latest.[1]

The track that went north from Hangard Copse, over the eastern end of Hill 99 and along the rim of Hangard Wood East defined most of 5 Brigade's objective and made the task look simple – deceptively so. Hangard Wood East was overlooked by the spur that separated it from Lancer Wood, so the advance had to finish on the spur for the wood to be secure. Though commanders look for distinct features when setting limits of exploitation, stopping at the track, therefore, was unwise. Hangard Wood East was also marked 'Underwood (Close)' on trench maps, signifying dense undergrowth. Off the rides, movement was exhausting and hard to control.

Starting below the spur between the two woods, the ravine Foch mentioned ran down to the Luce past Hill 99, Cemetery Copse, Hangard Cemetery and, on the far side, the big spur that screened Aubercourt. 6/Northants had straddled it on 4 April but now the ravine gave the Germans a sheltered approach for counterattacks on Hangard Wood East. While fire from the Aubercourt spur covered them and raked the wood, they could also form up in the finger re-entrant that branched off to skirt the wood's southern edge along aptly named Strip Copse. Gaining more ground on Hill 99, which overlooked both the ravine and the re-entrant and stood as a counterweight to the Aubercourt spur, would offset the advantages the Germans had.

Because all four of 5 Brigade's battalions were needed to hold a line 6,000 yards long, the assault force had to be light and was therefore widely spread across the 2,500-yard attack frontage. B Company, 19 Battalion would clear the upper half of Hangard Wood East, while D and C Companies secured the left flank by establishing platoon posts on the track at U.11.b.9.0 and U.12.a.1.9. C Company, 20 Battalion was to attack the lower half, while A Company guarded the right flank with a platoon post near U.23.d.3.6, the crossroads on Hill 99 midway between Hangard and Strip Copses. Aerial reconnaissance reports that Hangard Wood East was not strongly held had influenced the plan. In fact, two battalions from the 24th (Saxon) Reserve Division occupied it, II/133 RIR in the north and III/133 RIR in the south, each of which had strung two companies along the western edge facing the Australians.[2]

The Attack

Forming up behind the Villers-Bretonneux-Hangard road, the assault companies shivered as more rain made an already cold morning bitter. Many men still fell asleep. All reports described the opening barrage at 4.55 am as 'ragged'. Nothing landed in front of B Company but several shells lobbed onto C Company. The two companies were out of touch when they stepped off at 5.20 am towards Hangard Wood East, 500 yards away.

Waking to find that B Company had left, Lieutenant Percy Storkey, its second-in-command, sprinted to catch up as unseen machine guns wreaked havoc. When he arrived, more than a quarter of the company,

Hangard Wood East, Strip Copse, the ravine and Lancer Wood as seen from the Hill 99 crossroads.

Hangard Wood East   Strip Copse   D23   Lancer Wood   Ravine

including its commander, had been hit and the rest were continuing in isolated groups. A party of eleven men under Storkey was among the first to plunge into the thick undergrowth. Thrashing through the upper end of the wood, where a gap existed in the German line, they burst onto the main north-south ride. On the western side of it, twenty yards behind them, the two forward companies of II/133 RIR were flaying those still in the open.

When the closest Germans heard the Australians and turned around, Storkey shouted charge 'as if the whole battalion were following'. Taken by surprise and unsure whether the tiny band was indeed the vanguard of a larger force, the Germans were routed. Storkey won the Victoria Cross, his citation stating in part that his 'small party' charged 'with fixed bayonets, driving the enemy out, killing and wounding about thirty, and capturing three officers and fifty men, also one machine gun'.

It was a close run thing. As there would be no second chance, the initial onslaught had to shock the Germans into surrendering. Pausing to reload was out of the question, so the Australians used their rifle butts as well as their bayonets. Several German dead were found later with their skulls smashed in. The furthest Germans were reluctant to surrender and just had to swing round a machine gun to obliterate their attackers. Only after Storkey shot three and his men grenaded others did they put their hands up.

With II/133 RIR's forward line gone, the rest of B Company scrambled to the eastern edge of the wood unopposed. Germans off to the right and left immediately engaged it

Lieutenant Percy Storkey VC.

while II/133 RIR's depth companies on the crest 400 yards away geared up to counterattack. As the intended line on the track was clearly untenable, Storkey had no option but to order a withdrawal.

73

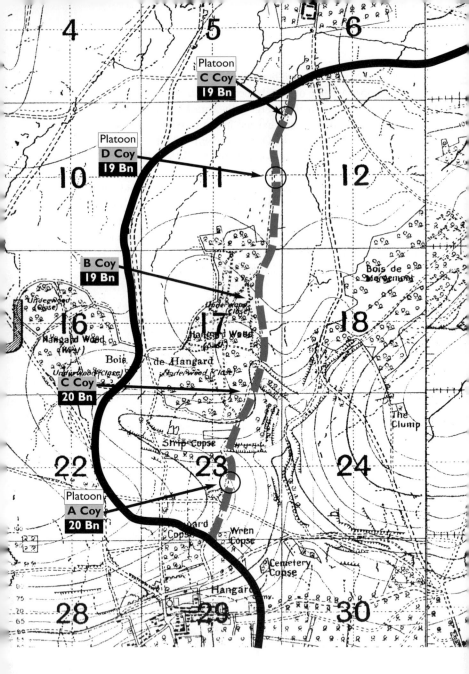

The Australian attack on Hangard Wood East on 7 April 1918.

Only the platoon posts on the track to the north, which had been established with little resistance, stayed in place.

C Company, 20 Battalion got through the southern part of the wood more easily because III/133 RIR's forward companies were thinly spread. Enfiladed on the far side by machine guns on the Aubercourt spur, it survived by staying well inside the tree line. The platoon advancing across Hill 99 to the crossroads had no cover whatsoever and was hurled back to its start point on the Cachy-Hangard road. The Germans could now move unimpeded along the ravine and the Strip Copse re-entrant.

III/133 RIR's two depth companies stormed out of the re-entrant at 6 am and quickly overran C Company's right flank. Two of 5 Machine Gun Company's guns, sited behind the wood, stopped them enveloping the rest of it. An hour later, two companies from I/133 RIR, which had poured over the Aubercourt spur, assembled in the ravine for a frontal assault but the Australian Lewis gunners twice broke them up. Baulked there, the Germans crossed the ravine further south and emplaced machine guns on the crossroads that the platoon from A Company was unable to reach. They covered a steady infiltration behind C Company from the head of the re-entrant.

Realising the situation was hopeless, Captain Victor Portman, the company commander and only officer left, withdrew the survivors to the track along the western edge of the wood, where the chalk pit on the southwestern corner at U.17.c.2.0 made a convenient headquarters. Mounting casualties, Portman among them, forced a withdrawal to the original front line after dark. What was termed a minor operation cost

The southwestern corner of Hangard Wood East, which became the headquarters of C Company, 20 Battalion.

the two battalions 151 men, a severe loss considering the small numbers involved.

Though Generals Butler and Lee blamed the reverse on enfilading machine guns from the southern bank of the Luce, even a cursory look at the map showed that they were too far away to interfere. The real causes were the miniscule size of the assault force given its task, the feeble barrage and, above all, the choice of an objective for 19 Battalion that proved untenable. C.E.W. Bean rightly called the attack 'a particularly interesting example of the way in which an operation, readily sketched in with a sweep of the pencil by higher authority, and formulated in a fluent order', ended up with a harassed company commander trying to achieve the impossible. The only saving grace was that 133 RIR had been so badly knocked about that it missed the subsequent fighting at Hangard.[3]

The Germans Attack

Despite the failure, the joint Franco-British offensive was set down for 9 April. The French First Army would recapture Moreuil and Moreuil Wood, while the Fourth Army was to seize the Aubercourt spur, thereby regaining Hangard Wood East and Lancer Wood. 175 Brigade from the still arriving 58th Division, which would be on the left of the attack, relieved 17 and 18 Battalions from 5 Brigade astride the railway, releasing them for the main role on the right. Loaned by 9 Brigade, 34 and 36 Battalions relieved the 19th and 20th, which were to form 5 Brigade's reserve and secure its flank respectively. When the French were not ready, the operation was postponed to 10 April.

The Germans got in beforehand with two attacks on 9 April, one

Hangard château, the scene of heavy fighting on 12 April 1918

massive, the other minor. First, *Georgette* began on the Lys. Haig rushed the 1st Australian Division, which had just reached the Somme, back to Flanders causing Rawlinson, in turn, to call off his own undertaking except for 5 Brigade's part, which had to proceed in order to protect the French left. Second, the 24th Reserve Division struck on the Luce, elements of 104 and 107 RIR capturing Hangard Cemetery and part of the village. A French counterattack ejected them but the dislocation forced yet another postponement of the joint offensive to 13 April. Nor were the Germans finished yet.

The grave of Lieutenant Colonel John Milne, Heath Cemetery.

At 6 am on 12 April an intense bombardment, heavily laced with smoke, fell between Hangard Wood West and Hangard, blinding 36 Battalion on Hill 99. The shelling ceased an hour later and as the smoke cleared, the Australians saw twin assaults converging on Hangard, above which an SOS rocket soared. Responding instantly, the French artillery pounded the ravine in front, annihilating 104 RIR, which had streamed southwestwards into it from Lancer Wood. Attacking along the Luce, 107 RIR had better luck, taking Hangard Copse, which dominated the village, and Hangard apart from its château.

Positioned 1,500 yards in rear, 7/RW Kents counterattacked alongside the French at 10.15 am. Half of the assault company wavered when engaged en route and the rest entrenched forty yards from the western edge of the copse. The French failed to reach Hangard. Another joint attempt employing 10/Essex, then in Gentelles, was planned for 7.20 pm. At 1.10 pm a German 5.9-inch shell slammed into 36 Battalion's headquarters, a slit trench at U.21.a.4.6. on the Cachy-Hangard road about half a mile from the Kents' old location. Lieutenant Colonel Milne, the hero of the battle on April 4, was killed instantly.

At 6.30 pm, 107 RIR finally took Hangard château. Half an hour later, the French began their bombardment of Hangard, and 10/Essex assembled at the head of the re-entrant that descends to Domart. The

Germans started shelling the advance but it pressed steadily on despite having 1000 yards to go. By 8.40 pm, the Essex had recaptured Hangard Copse in what the 18th Division's history rightly called 'a well-conducted little triumph'. The French regained the village, although 107 RIR remained in the cemetery and its copse. Towards midnight, 17 and 18 Battalions relieved the 34th and 36th on Hill 99. Dawn gave the 17th its first glimpse of the Hangard area:

> We were all amazed to discover that a cow was wandering about in No Man's Land. Rifle and machine-gun fire was continually passing over her head but she went on peacefully munching away, not in the least concerned. We made up our minds that as soon as it became dark we would try and get her in. But, unfortunately, our search party failed to locate her. So we assumed that the Jerries had stolen a march on us and had beaten us to it.[4]

The Cemetery and the Copse

As a result of the fighting on 12 April, the Franco-British offensive scheduled for next day was cancelled. Until the Germans were turfed out of Hangard Cemetery and Cemetery Copse, however, Hangard was at risk because they screened the approach along the Luce that 107 RIR had exploited so well. On the night of 13 April, wet and cold as usual, a patrol from A Company, 18 Battalion found Cemetery Copse to be strongly held. So the commanding officer, Lieutenant Colonel George Murphy, was lukewarm when Smith sounded him out at 9 am next morning about an attack on the copse in conjunction with a French attempt on the cemetery.

Smith was now answering to the commander of the 58th Division, Major General Albermarle Cator, who had relieved Lee of responsibility for the line south of the Roman Road. He saw the operation as a preliminary to the pinching out of Hangard Wood East. Not surprisingly, Murphy was ordered at 3.45 pm on 14 April to capture Cemetery Copse and the strongpoint on the Hill 99 crossroads, now manned by 104 RIR, the battalion which had shot up Captain Portman's men a week earlier. The attack would go in at 3 am next morning, preceded by the establishment of three posts on Hill 99 as soon as possible after midnight to prevent interference from 133 RIR in Hangard Wood East.

By 1.30 am, B Company, 18 Battalion had occupied unseen the two northerly posts at U.22.b.7.6 and U.22.b.9.1 but exactly what happened concerning the largest post, which Lieutenant Harold Thompson's platoon was to set up at U.23.c.5.8, remains obscure. Reconnoitring beforehand, Thompson discovered that the Germans had also put a strongpoint on the Villers-Bretonneux-Hangard Road crossroads, which was 200 yards southwest of where his platoon was headed. Lieutenant Norman McLaren's platoon, also from B Company, was to form up near this crossroads for its assault on the main crossroads post 500 yards east at 3 am. In view of what unfolded, Thompson may have decided to wait until then and, ignoring his own objective, attack the westerly crossroads in order to give McLaren a clear run at the easterly one.

In the event, McLaren's platoon was caught in the light of a flare twenty-five yards from the main strongpoint and twenty-three of its thirty men were hit, including McLaren. Finding the Germans on the westerly crossroads asleep, Thompson's platoon went through their dugouts with bomb and bayonet. The survivors fled, except for the occupant of a missed dugout who mortally wounded Thompson. Crossing the ravine, the German supports on the Aubercourt spur started to arrive at 4.15 am. At daybreak, an officer was heard shouting out attack orders and the platoon, almost surrounded, withdrew.

Closer to Hangard, A Company under Lieutenant Victor Frewin had crept along the sunken road above the village, which was the boundary with the French, and formed up 200 yards from Cemetery Copse. Ten minutes after the bombardment began, they advanced, brushed through an outpost line and divided into three groups on reaching it. Fired on from the northern edge, Lieutenant Rupert Gascoigne-Roy's party charged and about forty Germans surrendered. The groups going through the copse and around the southern edge met little opposition and, together with Gascoigne-Roy's men, dug three posts about fifty yards beyond the eastern side. He took command when Frewin was killed while trying to locate a long overdue carrying party with defence stores.

A Company's attack had ended barely twenty yards from I/107 RIR's headquarters. Its commander threw orderlies, batmen and anyone else on hand at the copse. Though the counterattack failed, it revealed how thinly spread the Australians were and the Germans concentrated machine gun and trench mortar fire on them, making

A Company, 18 Battalion, attacked Cemetery Copse (*right*) from Hangard Copse (*left*). The view is northwards from Hangard Communal Cemetery Extension.

Hangard Copse

Cemetery Copse

movement impossible. Gascoigne-Roy saw the carrying party finally appear, only to be carved up forty yards from the northern edge of the copse, and was hit in the head and leg trying to lead it in. A second party was also forced to turn back. When the southern post fell silent at 6.25 am, the left and centre posts had already been overrun. Though the French took the cemetery, contact with them was never possible.

Apart from the two northerly posts, 18 Battalion's line was unchanged and 84 of the 180 attackers were casualties. General Cator generously praised 5 Brigade's efforts:

> *All the fighting work they did here was splendid . . . I have never had the good luck to be with Australians in this war, but I think I can safely say that they are quite one of the best fighting units I have come across.*

But the fact was that 5 Brigade had lost heavily in a series of local actions that were poorly planned and directed at objectives of questionable value. The men knew it and their morale, sky-high a week or so earlier, sagged. When they were relieved by 173 Brigade on 19 April and returned to the 2nd Division, absence without leave increased. By then the ravine was known as Death Valley.[5]

Frustration

The fighting around Hangard constituted the third phase of the defence of Villers-Bretonneux and Amiens. Trying though it was for the Australians, it also troubled Rawlinson by underlining the fragility of his right flank. By mid-April there was still no sign of the promised French attack to clear the Avre, which would make it less vulnerable. His patience exhausted, Rawlinson told Haig that the French did nothing but promise:

> *I have discussed this question with the III Corps Commander and his Divisional Commanders, and they are all agreed that unless something is done by the French to restore the situation on the right it may become serious and the safety of Amiens compromised.*

Haig complained to Foch and on 18 April the French First Army finally attacked. As the British Official History pointedly remarks, it was the first offensive action taken by the French to relieve the British since the fighting began on the 21st March. Even then, it was carried out by little more than a division and was only partly successful, gaining just 500 yards on average. Still, the Bois de Sénécat was recaptured, depriving the Germans of their observation over Amiens and making Rawlinson's right more secure.[6]

Fortification

On the Somme flank, Major General Hobbs had instructed 14 and 15 Brigades on 6 April to gain more room on Hill 104. By means of aggressive patrolling, the 15th advanced its line towards Hamel in nightly bounds of 500 yards and had reached Bouzencourt when it went into reserve at Blangy-Tronville on 9 April, relieved by 8 Brigade. Using stealth, or 'peaceful penetration' as the Australians called it, 14 Brigade snatched posts between Vaire Wood and the Roman Road.

Much of the old front line on Hill 104 became the support line, and a reserve line, later called the Villers System, was dug from the Roman Road on the eastern outskirts of Villers-Bretonneux across the reverse slope behind it. What eventually became the Villers Switch

Major General Talbot Hobbs.

was scratched out from the railway at O.28.a across the lip of the hollow north of the town. More exposed and on the periphery of the Hangard Wood fighting, the line south of the Roman Road remained largely as the battle on April 4 had left it. Battalion headquarters in the fields were risky places because there were no existing deep dugouts and converging tracks betrayed their locations. Milne was not the first casualty. Lieutenant Colonel David McConaghy, an original Anzac, a veteran of Lone Pine and an inspirational figure at the dreadful battle of Fromelles in July 1916, died on 9 April when 54 Battalion's headquarters on Hill 104 was pulped.

Work continued on the Gentelles/Aubigny Line and the Cachy Switch, and three other defence lines had been started behind them. The first, 1,500 yards further back was the Bois Line (also called the Sydney System), which began in front of the Bois Gentelles and ran to the Somme via the Bois de Blangy. Another 2,500 yards rearwards, the Blangy-Tronville Line stretched from that village to St Nicolas, part of Boves today. The Bois Switch ran eastwards from it to the Bois Line, and the Glisy-Blangy Switch went westwards from it for a mile along the Villers-Bretonneux railway to the Boves-Glisy Line. Extending from Glisy to the other railway north of Boves, it was the last line of defence before Amiens. If these systems looked convincing on maps, the reality was different, for the troops were too few and too tired to develop them. The trenches were shallow and the wire was 'very poor', wrote the British Official Historian.[7]

Gas

In Villers-Bretonneux, almost every building – including the red and white chateaux – was damaged and the eastern half of the town practically demolished. The destruction stunned the Australian War Correspondent, Frank Cutlack:

> It was a most horrible ruin, a revolting sight of torn and gutted houses and littered streets, littered too with dead here and there among the splintered glass, smouldering beams and heaps of bricks. It was worse than a town obliterated – like Ypres for example. Ypres was a bleached skeleton; Villers was being mutilated in death.[8]

On 16 April, the French captured a Bavarian who revealed that the town would be attacked that day but nothing happened until next 4 am next morning when the Germans began soaking the triangle it made with the Bois d'Aquenne and Cachy with gas. Villers-Bretonneux and the wood were drenched, shells landing on them at the rate of one every two seconds at several stages of the three-hour bombardment.

Villers-Bretonneux on the way to becoming a ruin.

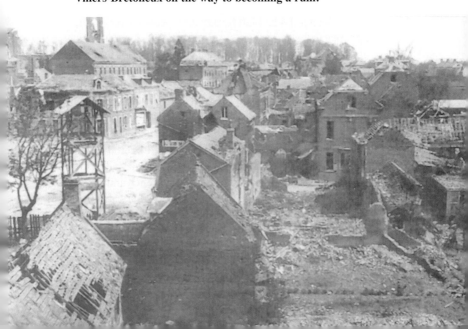

Australian gas casualties.

8/Londons lost eighty-four men in one of the cellars being used as a shelter. Forgetting that the environs were dripping with toxic chemicals, other troops removed their respirators as soon as the shelling ceased and casualties leapt. Morshead was among the 271 in 33 Battalion, which had to be relieved by the 36th. Over 300 victims came from 14 Brigade and almost 800 from the 58th Division.

Reorganization

The gas attack interrupted a reorganisation of the Villers-Bretonneux front that had begun on 13 April. Until then, the Somme had been the boundary between the Australian Corps and III Corps, a clumsy arrangement because the emergencies south of the river had necessitated Australian brigades being cross-grouped in British divisions and the 5th Australian Division replacing the 14th (Light) Division in III Corps. North of the river, the 8th Division, a British formation, had replaced the 1st Division in the Australian Corps on its departure for Flanders. At Haig's direction, Rawlinson now made the Australian Corps solely responsible for the Somme. Returning to its parent formation, the 5th Division slipped northwards astride the river, so that its defence fell to just one divisional headquarters. In turn, on 18 April, 8th Division was transferred to III Corps. The Division was to hold Villers-Bretonneux, by the same date, 58 Division's arrival had been completed.

Crossing the Villers-Bretonneux-Hamel road at P.20.c.0.8, the inter-corps boundary left 14 Brigade on the northern end of Hill 104. On 20 April, 25 Brigade from the 8th Division occupied the 1,300 yards to the Roman Road with 2/Rifle Brigade and 2/E. Lancs, and held 2/R.

Berks above the hollow north of the town and on Hill 104 for counterattacks. 24 Brigade had relieved 174 Brigade south of the Roman Road the night before. 2/Northants and 1/Sherwood Foresters were left and right of the railway and 1/Worcs had the counterattack role. 2/Devons assumed garrison duties in the town when 23 Brigade relieved Rosenthal's brigade there. 22/Durham Light Infantry (DLI), the divisional pioneers at Blangy-Tronville, worked on the Aubigny Line. On the right of the 8th Division, the three battalions of 173 Brigade – 2/4, 2/2 and 3/Londons – manned the 58th Division's front line from north to south.

Deployed in depth, 9 and 12/Londons from 175 Brigade were in the Gentelles Line behind Cachy, with 2/10 Londons near the village as the counterattack battalion to the 173rd. 174 Brigade was in divisional reserve at Cagny, six miles west. 53 and 54 Brigades from the 18th Division were near Amiens except for two companies of 6/Northants and a few odds and ends, together known as Shepherd's Force after their commander, Major S.F. Shepherd, which protected Cachy itself. Seven field artillery brigades supported the front line divisions, which could also call on III Corps' eight-nine heavy guns. Butler had available as well A Company, 1 Tank Battalion's thirteen Mark IV tanks and seven light Whippets from X Company, 3 Tank Battalion. Apart from three Mark IV's held in the Bois d'Aquenne under the 8th Division, he kept the armour in the Bois de Blangy for counterattacks between Cachy and Gentelles.

With seven battalions forward and the rest distributed in a layered defence, Butler's dispositions seemed solid when the reorganisation was completed on 21 April. On the following night, though, 2/E. Lancs had to relieve 2/Devons, who were feeling the effects of the gas in Villers-Bretonneux. To avoid a repetition, the Lancs' companies were strung out around the eastern rim of the town, leaving 25 Brigade's front line held by one battalion, 2/Rifle Brigade, instead of two. Butler also lacked a formed body of troops for an immediate counterattack on a large-scale and his formations were still below fighting condition.

The 8th Division was new to III Corps. Formed from regular units recalled from imperial garrison duties at the start of the war, it was decimated at Fromelles in May 1915, fifteen months before the 5th Australian Division met the same fate on the same ground. It was clobbered again at Ovillers on the Somme on 1 July 1916. Since then, it had done well enough to be one of the first three British divisions that, along with the Dominion ones, received additional Lewis guns when the allocation was doubled at the start of 1918. Of the brigade commanders, Brigadier General Clifford Coffin of the 25th had won the VC at Westhoek at the start of Third Ypres and George Grogan would win it whilst leading 23 Brigade on the Aisne in May 1918. The adjutant of 2/Northants, Captain Hubert Essame, wrote of the divisional commander, Major General William Heneker:

> *He expected to be saluted by everyone within eye range; his eagle eye could detect an unshaven chin, the need for a haircut, a grease stain, or an unpolished button, at a considerable distance. His comments were clear, vividly expressed and long remembered.*

Though the 8th Division had fought hard during the March Retreat and in the Moreuil Wood battles, the cost was half its infantry: 250 officers and 4,693 men. 2/Middlesex and 2/W. Yorks, the worst hit battalions, each received drafts of about a dozen officers and 700 men, and 22/DLI 450, whose physique was 'much below average'. The lack of time to assimilate and train these replacements was a familiar problem.

Indeed, Rawlinson remarked that III Corps was made up of 'children', but he had to make do with them for as long as British priorities were focussed on containing *Georgette*. The stark contrast between the Australians and Butler's troops highlighted the quandary Rawlinson was in. He had publicly staked his reputation on keeping Villers-Bretonneux but III Corps, not the Australians, were defending it.[9]

Anticipation

The Australians pitied the youngsters but were more concerned that the town might well be lost, in which case the Australian flank on Hill 104 would be turned. None was more worried than Elliott. Although 15 Brigade was in reserve at Blangy-Tronville, he kept a battalion at constant readiness at the southern end of the Aubigny Line in the Bois l'Abbé, a mile behind Villers-

Brigadier General Clifford Coffin.

Brigadier General George Grogan.

Major General William Heneker.

Bretonneux. He also prepared contingency plans for a brigade counterattack and had terrain models made for his staff and commanders to study. His anxiety increased after the gas bombardment made the Bois d'Aquenne uninhabitable, and the tanks in it withdrew to the Bois l'Abbé. When 22/DLI at Blangy-Tronville sent a single platoon to relieve his battalion in the wood, it was the last straw.

Elliott convinced Hobbs to have the 5th Division's pioneers dig a long trench westwards from the Aubigny Line towards Blangy-Tronville. Ostensibly for 'communications', it was in fact a switch to protect the flank of 57 and 58 Battalions at the northern end of the Aubigny Line if the British were ejected from the Bois l'Abbé. At Blangy-Tronville, 59 and 60 Battalions stood by to counterattack Villers-Bretonneux. Patrols from both battalions were to go to the town at the first sign of a German attack in order to keep Elliott informed of the situation. Hobbs also ordered the digging of Pioneer Trench, a switch that ran from the right of his front line to the Aubigny Line. When work started on 23 April, every man knew that another attack was imminent.

Early on 22 April, 1/Sherwood Foresters had captured a sergeant major from the 4th Guards Division, who revealed that it had just relieved the 9th BR Division at Marcelcave for an attack at 3 am next day. Aerial reconnaissance on the 23rd found Hangard Wood crowded with troops and detected some 'little square objects, thought to be wagons with trench-mortar ammunition'. Gas deluged the British rear areas during the afternoon. That night 2/2 and 2/4 Londons each picked up an Alsatian deserter from the 77th Reserve Division, newly arrived from Russia, who said that 'storm divisions' had taken over the line opposite and would assault after a two and a half hour bombardment, mainly with gas, early next morning. Shedding light on the 'little square objects', they disclosed that fifteen tanks were to spearhead the attack, which had been twice postponed. The French captured a gunner from the Guards Ersatz Division who confirmed their story.[10]

Incredibly, 23 Brigade was relieving the 24th on the right of the 8th Division's line when the latest information came in. 2/Middlesex and 2/W. Yorks replaced 2/Northants and 1/Sherwood Foresters respectively, and 2/Devons took up counterattack duties at the head of the Cachy Switch after a brief rest at Blangy-Tronville. Apart from two companies of 1/Worcs that joined Shepherd's Force, 24 Brigade went back to the Gentelles and Blangy-Tronville Lines as the 8th Division's reserve. Perhaps Heneker went ahead with the relief because the warning of an attack on 23 April had proven to be a false alarm. Whatever the reason, it left 23 Brigade in the same position as the 14th (Light) Division on the morning of 4 April: facing an attack without having seen in daylight the ground it was to defend.

Plan of Attack

Ludendorff's main aim in renewing the attack was to divert attention from Flanders, where a last attempt to capture strategically important Mount Kemmel would hopefully revive ailing *Georgette*. Straightening out the salient driven into the French line south of the Luce was his secondary aim. As they did before the 4 April attack, his commanders felt they had insufficient resources and gained a few days' postponement to rest their formations. The operation was also scaled down. In its final form, the Second Army sought to gain the line Villers-Bretonneux-Cachy-Domart-Bertaucourt-Thennes (on the Luce-Avre confluence a mile west of Domart) but exploitation beyond it would occur if the main objective, Villers-Bretonneux, fell. At the very least, the Germans hoped to get their artillery still closer to Amiens.

XIV Corps would again assault Villers-Bretonneux, the 228th Division on the Roman Road with 207 RIR on the left, 48 IR on the right, and II/35 Fusilier in support attacking it from the north, east and southeast, and the 4th Guards, on the far side of the railway with 93 RIR and 5 Guard Grenadier on right and left, attacking it from the

A German A7V tank leaves the railhead for the battle area.

southeast and south. On linking in the town, the 4th Guards would go for the Bois d'Aquenne, while the 228th swung onto Hill 104 in conjunction with frontal assaults on it by 478 and 479 IR of the 243rd Division. In XI Corps, the 77th Reserve Division would seize Hangard Wood West before pressing on to Cachy, and the 208th Division was to capture Hill 99, Hangard and its copse before heading to Berteaucourt with the Guards Ersatz Division. XXIII Reserve Corps north of the Somme would launch a diversionary raid an hour before the assault. On the southern flank, the 13th Division from LI Corps was to mount a small attack west of the Avre. The 19th, 9th BR and Jäger Divisions were in reserve.

The thirteen serviceable A7V tanks were divided into three groups. Three tanks under Lieutenant Skopnik would advance with the 228th Division north of the railway directly against Villers-Bretonneux. Six more, commanded by Lieutenant Uihlein, were to support the 4th Guards south of the railway between the town and Cachy, and the remaining four under Lieutenant Steinhardt would move with 77th Reserve Division against Cachy itself. With its slab armour hanging down over the tracks like a crinoline skirt, each tank weighed thirty tons, boasted a 57-mm gun and six Maxims, and had a crew of eighteen. They were in inferior in cross-country mobility to British tanks, but the unspoilt and obstacle-free terrain south of the Roman Road was ideal for them.

NOTES

1. *OH*, p. 501.
2. Bn Order 76, 6 April 1918, 19 Bn WD, Item 23/36, Roll 52; Bn Order 40, 6 April, 20 Bn WD, Item 23/37, Roll 53; all in AWM 4.
3. Report dated 7 April in 20 Bn WD; 5 Bde, 'Report on Operation at Hangard Wood' dated 7 April 1918, 5 Bde WD; *OH*, p. 501.
4. Nichols, op. cit., p. 319; H.G. Taylor, *The Mob That Shot The Camel*, MSS0863, AWM, p. 145.
5. Reports dated 15-16 April 1918, 18 Bn WD, Item 23/35, Roll 51, AWM; *OH*, p. 521; K.W. Mackenzie, *The Story of the Seventeenth Battalion AIF in The Great War* (privately published, 1946), pp. 226-7.
6. P. Simkins, 'For Better or Worse: Sir Henry Rawlinson and his Allies in 1916 and 1918' in M. Hughes and M. Seligmann (eds.), *Leadership in Conflict* (Leo Cooper, 2000), p. 23; *Military Operations II*, p. 366.
7. *Military Operations II*, p. 385.
8. Cutlack, op. cit., p. 122.
9. H. Essame, *The Battle for Europe 1918* (Scribners, 1972); J.H. Boraston and C.E.O. Bax, *The Eighth Division 1914-1918* (Medici Society, 1926), p. 199; 22/DLI WD, 4 April 1918, WO 95/1702, TNA; Maurice, op. cit., pp. 217-8; *OH*, p. 536.
10. *OH*, p. 534.

Chapter Six

VILLERS-BRETONNEUX LOST

At 3.45 am on 24 April, as the early morning fog grew denser with the approaching dawn, a tremendous bombardment fell between Hill 104 and the Bois de Sénécat. The front line, Villers-Bretonneux, the Cachy Switch, and the surrounding woods, roads and villages were all clobbered. Heavily flavoured with gas, the shelling was the heaviest the 18th Division ever experienced. Lieutenant F.S. Mason was caught with 2/Northants in the Bois l'Abbé:

> We looked towards the line and through the trees a sudden flickering was seen, like summer lightning. Like a sudden thundershower, the wood was drenched with all kinds of shell, including gas. 'Get the men out into the open', shouted the company commander. Where the hell are the men? Where is that trench with No. 7 platoon in? I find, in the confusion and bursting shells, falling trenches and trees that I haven't the foggiest notion of where my platoon is and run about in circles.[1]

At 4.30 am, 85 IR attacked 29 Battalion on the northern bank of the Somme and was easily seen off. The Australians knew that it was a feint because of the bombardment going in south of the river. At about 5.30 am the Germans substituted smoke for gas in their shelling of the front line. Visibility was atrocious when the assault began on the four-mile frontage between Hangard and the right of 54 Battalion, 1,300 yards north of the Roman Road, at 6 am.

British troops in the Bois l'Abbé.

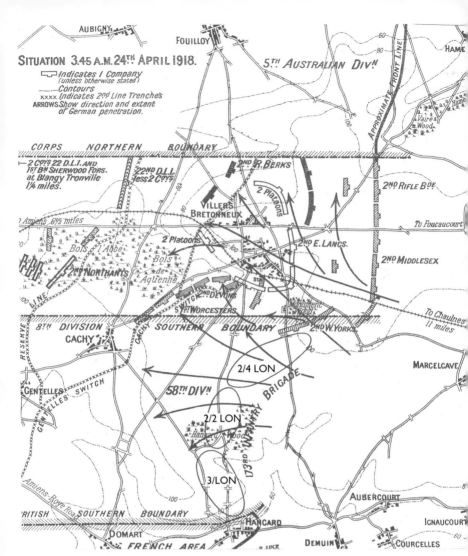

The German attack on III Corps on 24 April 1918.

The infantry were supposed to lead but, in practice, the tanks did. 'It seems their role was to cross our front line, move up and down the trenches, destroy the defenders, and prepare the way for the infantry to advance later', remarked the 8th Division's War Diary. Seeing the tanks lumber out of the gloom onto their positions horrified the young British soldiers, who had no effective anti-tank weapons. They broke wherever the tanks appeared. Infantry with flamethrowers mopped up the remnants. As luck would have it, the attack fell heaviest on 23 Brigade, which had first glimpsed its front line in daylight at the same time as the Germans did.[2]

23 Brigade

Strung out between the far end of the airfields on the Roman Road and the railway bridge at V.1.b.5.6, 2/Middlesex on the left of 23 Brigade had already been badly mauled by the bombardment. When it lifted, B and A Companies, on the right and centre, saw the tanks of Lieutenant Skopnik's section thirty yards away. *Lotti* and *Alter Fritz*, commanded by Lieutenants Vietze and Volkheim respectively, trundled up to the front line trench, machine guns blazing, and enfiladed it. Skopnik's tank was just behind them with 207 RIR's flamethrowers. Casualties were again crippling and many of the survivors surrendered. Located with his depth platoon 120 yards in rear, Captain Brodie, B Company's commander was lucky not be among them:

> *The writer's first intimation of the attack was a sudden, accurate and deadly fire on his support platoon, and practically simultaneously he heard his front line open fire. The nature of this machine-gun fire was unusual; it raked the parapet, and any man who put his head up was shot down immediately . . . Suddenly the machine-gun fire ceased, the writer put his head up and saw an enormous and terrifying iron pill-box, bristling with automatic weapons, bearing straight down on him. He lay down in the trench on top of a diminutive sergeant . . . and the German tank, for such as it was, passed right over them. The writer thought that his end had come at last, but after seeing the tracks of the tank pass about 3 feet above his face, he got up, turned round and fired a .32 automatic pistol at the water jacket of the machine-gun at the stern of the tank.*
>
> *Looking over the parapet the writer saw a second tank*

Map from the 2/Middlesex War Diary showing dispositions before the German attack.

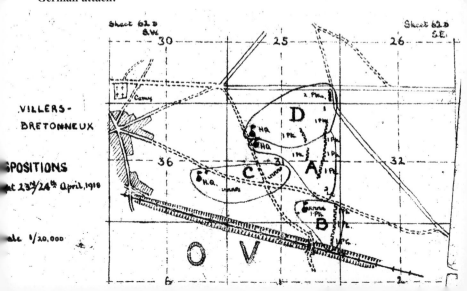

proceeding along his front line trench, not crossing it, but running along it from end to end. The men of the front trench were either shot down in the trench, crushed, or shot down as they jumped out of it. In the latter case they were shot at both by the tank machine-guns and by the German light automatic gunners, who had taken up a position some twenty-five to thirty yards from the trench. In addition, the left forward platoon was swept by fire from a flammenwerfer, and dense volumes of black smoke rose close to them.

Having dealt with the front line trench, the second tank turned and made for the writer's trench, and a third tank appeared, followed by German riflemen. The riflemen proceeded to bayonet those men left in the front line trench, and the third tank then began to turn down the writer's trench from end to end. The writer, acting on the assumption that 'he who fights and runs away, lives to fight another day', did not wait to be crushed to death but took to his heels, making for the railway-cutting with his little sergeant and the remnants of his men. All except five were shot down by the second and third tanks.[3]

Withdrawing along the railway, what was left of 2/Middlesex regrouped in the Gentelles Line in the Bois l'Abbé.

Realising on reaching the D23 bridge that he had outstripped the infantry, Skopnik turned his tank around and cleaned up four Lewis guns manned by C Company in depth. When the infantry caught up, he headed along the railway embankment, leading them to the northwestern outskirts of Villers-Bretonneux and trampling the machine guns of 2/E. Lancs as he went. Around 7.45 am, Skopnik returned to the eastern edge of the town and joined Vietze and Volkheim at the brickworks in O.36.d, a site in the modern industrial zone occupied by the Airplast/Proust complex. Visibility had improved to about 100 yards by then, enabling the three tanks to work together. They took the rest of C Company and some of 2/E. Lancs, which had been resisting stubbornly there, in flank and rear.

Once A and B Companies had started to crumble, III/48 IR hooked around the right of D Company on the Roman Road and cut it off. 15 Platoon under 2/Lieutenant Martin held out on the road itself until only six men, including him, were left. All that remained of D Company, they withdrew northwest to join 2/R. Berks on Hill 104, giving I/48 IR an easy passage towards the northern side of Villers-Bretonneux.

Split into two troops of three tanks, each with small parties of 93 RIR following fifty yards behind them, Lieutenant Uihlein's group

The ground over which Lieutenant Uihlein's tanks attacked 2/W. Yorks as seen through the mist from the D23 near Monument Farm.

struck neighbouring 2/W. Yorks. Like the Middlesex, it had three companies forward, C Company on the railway and A and B Companies stretching in a tight perimeter around Monument Wood and Farm to the D23 crossroads in U.6.c. As the Battalion War Diary records, the action was no different to the one occurring simultaneously on the other side of the track: 'The heavy fire opened by the men against the tanks had little effect and they came up to the line and fired up and down the posts with MG and the German infantry occupied the position'.

Hugging the railway cutting, Lieutenant Hennecke in *Baden I* led *Cyklop* and *Mephisto* through C Company. Hennecke and Lieutenant Burmann in *Cyklop* drove straight on but Lieutenant Theunissen in *Mephisto* skewed towards Monument Wood, wiping out C Company's flank before foundering in a shell crater. Attacking A and B Companies from the south and east, *Herkules*, *Gretchen* and Tank 541 of the second troop met stubborn resistance. A hail of fire wounded *Gretchen*'s driver just as overheating caused a breakdown. Lieutenant Lappe somehow restarted the tank and it returned to the German line. When brake and gearbox problems and a wounded driver stranded *Herkules*, Lieutenant Bartens and his crew briefly joined the infantry. They got going again after Tank 541 almost single-handedly took out the farm, knocking down one of its few remaining walls in the process.[4]

Outflanked by the loss of Monument Farm, D Company, in depth at the head of the hollow 36 Battalion had occupied on 4 April, withdrew to the Yorks' headquarters by the railway station. About 140 men were collected and a hasty defence organised but a tank, probably 541, approached the right flank and Hennecke's troop the centre. 207 RIR's snipers, who had followed Lieutenant Skopnik's tank through the town, began picking off the left. Retiring along the railway, the survivors formed a defensive flank with 2/E. Lancs on the western side of Villers-Bretonneux, just south of the railway bridge on the Roman Road at O.28.d.3.4. Heavy fire from 207 RIR in the town soon forced them north of the road.

2/Devons, 23 Brigade's counterattack battalion, were groggy after

93

being drenched by gas in the Cachy Switch. The two companies at the top end of it did not see 2/W. Yorks pulling back north of them or Tank 541 to their south. Lieutenant Colonel R.H. Anderson-Morshead was therefore among the first to know that his battalion was under attack when the tank crawled up to his headquarters at O.34.c.5.0, blew the parapet in and moved on. Some time later, *Baden I*, *Cyklop* and *Herkules* appeared in front of the two northern companies. They disintegrated, opening up a 1,400-yard gap between the two southern companies in the switch and the Lancs and Yorks northwest of the town.

Covered by the tanks, the German infantry headed into the Bois d'Aquenne. Going through the town, 93 RIR occupied the northern part of the wood on the Roman Road, and two companies of II/35 Fusilier plugged the gaps with 207 RIR near the bridge. The three battalions of 5 Guard Grenadier and two machine gun companies moved along the hollow to the southern part of the wood facing the Cachy Switch. Their line along the Fouilloy-Cachy road, today's D523, was the closest to Amiens that the Germans reached.[5]

25 Brigade

North of the Roman Road, the 243rd Division was not to launch a full-scale assault on Hill 104 before Villers-Bretonneux had fallen. Until then, it would merely maintain touch with the right of 228th Division's advance, a task for which tank support was deemed unnecessary. 25 Brigade initially faced, therefore, what amounted to a subsidiary attack by 478 IR, and 2/Rifle Brigade in the front line easily swept it away. Neighbouring 54 Battalion did the same to II/479 IR. Though the Germans called for heavy shelling of the hill, it was the collapse south of the Roman Road that eventually forced 2/Rifle Brigade back.

When III/48 RIR broke through on the right of 2/Middlesex, two companies continued northwards over the Roman Road. At 7 am, a runner informed Lieutenant Colonel H.S.C. Richardson that A and C

5 Guard Grenadier's advance past the southern side of Villers-Bretonneux.

Monument Wood · Lancer Wood · 5 Guard Grenadier

German tanks in Villers-Bretonneux.

Companies in the front line and D Company, in support near the crossroads in P.25.b, were being attacked in flank and rear. Hidden by the smoke and mist, the envelopment, combined with another frontal assault, killed or captured nearly every man. At 8 am Richardson reinforced B Company on the left with his headquarters and ordered it to pivot backwards in order to gain touch with 2/R. Berks, whose companies on Hill 104 had swung back towards the supports above the hollow north of Villers-Bretonneux. Together they formed a defensive flank from O22.d through O.24.central that faced southeast to counter any German attempt to debouch from the town. But it was weak and riddled with gaps.

After some house-to-house fighting on the eastern edge of the town involving *Lotti* and *Alter Fritz*, I/48 IR had reached the northern outskirts around 7.20 am. Joined by the rest of III/48 IR, it started the northerly assault on Hill 104 that comprised the second phase of the 228th Division's mission. But the German guns were unaware of the success of the first phase and their barrage in support of 478 IR plastered both battalions. They withdrew to the town's northern rim, where II/48 IR reinforced them. When 478 IR was finally able to move, it established a southwesterly chain of posts across Hill 104 to gain touch. The rest of II/35 Fusilier filled holes in the line.

Improving visibility ended any hope the Germans had of taking Hill

104. 14 Brigade had two battalions in depth on the western spur of the feature, the 56th curving around to face the town on the line of the infant Pioneer Switch, and the 55th on the northern slope. Between them, they covered all the roads from Villers-Bretonneux to Fouilloy, where 14 Brigade's headquarters was, and Aubigny. In addition, 14 Machine Gun Company's sixteen guns and some British machine guns were arrayed along the hill and around its flanks, and 25 Brigade's headquarters stood at O.17.c.3.3, where the Australian National Memorial is now.[6]

Of 25 Brigade's three battalions, tanks attacked only 2/E. Lancs, led by Lieutenant Colonel G.E.M. Hill. Deployed in a semi-circle around the eastern outskirts of Villers-Bretonneux for its last-ditch defence, the Lancs faced most of those that had punched through the battalions in the front line – in other words, the heaviest armoured assault of the battle. C Company on the right was overrun along with D Company, 2/W. Yorks. A and B Companies in the centre were also overwhelmed, although some men fought on in the brickworks and the town. Outflanked and isolated, the two platoons of D Company/2/E. Lancs on the left withdrew west of the town, where the other two platoons were in reserve south of the bridge on the Roman Road. 207 RIR's arrival on the northwestern outskirts necessitated another withdrawal at 9.30 am to the far side of the railway 350 yards from the bridge, where Hill collected about 100 men, including the W. Yorks. He wrote subsequently:

> *I had considerable difficulty in holding a line. There were no trenches of any sort . . . Just as things were looking rather blue, a very cheery [Australian] subaltern turned up with a patrol. His name was Christian.*

Lieutenants John Christian and Roy Callander led the two patrols from 59 Battalion, each of twenty men, that Elliott had sent out when the attack started. As instructed, they went initially to O.28.d.0.5, a location near the bridge on the Roman Road 150 yards ahead of Hill's men. Protected by the four surviving tanks of Lieutenant Uihlein's group, the Germans could be seen entering the Bois d'Aquenne, 93 RIR racing into it over the railway bridge on the western outskirts of the town at O.34.b.9.8 and 5 Guard Grenadier moving along the southern hollow. One tank, probably *Cyklop*, drove along the railway cutting to the bridge on the Roman Road, near which was Christian's right flank. Though sniping at the vision slits stopped it, he prudently decided to join Hill.

The Germans were then engaged by an 18-pounder from B Battery,

Australian machine gunners on Hill 104. Note how open the ground is.

83 Brigade RFA, which 2/Lieutenant A.I. Butler had moved onto the railway embankment on the western side of the railway bridge over the D523, 700 yards behind Hill's line. The infantry scattered, and the tanks shifted closer to the Bois d'Aquenne and out of view. Coming around the edge of the wood, one of them suddenly re-appeared at 9.45 am, 200 yards from Butler's position:

> *I had my gun slewed around. The tank still came on. Then when it was 100 yards away, our first round was fired. It fell short. The second round – percussion shrapnel – burst right on top of the tank. There was a large cloud of smoke, and the tank turned around and went into the dip again, just as our third round burst under its tail.*

Unable to extend south of the railway, Hill and Christian staked out a line that started from it at O.28.c.5.7, roughly opposite the rear of today's Adelaide Cemetery, and ran 350 yards north. The right flank bent back to face the Bois d'Aquenne while Callender's patrol secured the left by moving 500 yards northeast to the Aubigny-Villers-Bretonneux Road, where it combined with a platoon or so of 2/R. Berks at the northern hollow. Although the 2/W. Yorks survivors retired to the Gentelles Line, the E. Lancs and the Australians held on all day, watching the northwestern exits of the town and 'furnishing one element of certainty in an otherwise vague position'.[7]

173 Brigade

Unlike the ironing board flat terrain over which XIV Corps had advanced south of the Roman Road, much of the going in front of XI Corps further south was unsuitable for tanks. 3/Londons on Hill 99 shattered the right of the 208th Division, which attacked without them, and remained in position until the loss of Hangard by the French in the evening forced a limited withdrawal. 2/2 Londons on the Villers-Bretonneux road in front of Hangard Wood West repulsed the left of the 77th Reserve Division, which also had none. At 7 am, though, 2/2 Londons reported: 'Bosch through on left of our line with tanks and reported working round our left flank'. C Company, which had been in support, reinforced D Company there and B Company in the centre. At 7.40 am, D Company reported 'enemy in trench on left and are in support line, 300 yards to left rear. This is on 4th Bn front'. Contact with D and C Companies was lost as word arrived that B Company,

(Above) The bridge on the N29 at the western end of Villers-Bretonneux, which a German tank reached by driving along the railway.

(Right) The same view today.

and A Company on the right, were being enfiladed. Some idea of the situation emerged at 9.35 am:

> *My left Coy has fallen back, also my right and centre Coys, from verbal message. They are occupying positions on road running through U.16. & c., and 15.b. Position of 4th still obscure.*

The message meant that the 2/2nd, while still in touch with 3/Londons, had abandoned all but the southwestern corner of Hangard Wood West and swung back towards Cachy on the line of the Cachy-Hangard road because the Germans were through 2/4 Londons.

Because the tanks of Lieutenant Steinhardt's section fell behind while detouring around the badly torn up ground at Lancer Wood, 2/4 Londons had initially beaten off the right of the 77th Reserve Division with heavy losses. The tanks arrived in time for the next attempt at 7 am, and Lieutenant Colonel W.R.H Dann's description of it has a familiar ring:

> *Heavy rifle and machine-gun fire was opened on these tanks without effect. The tanks after some little time managed to get astride our front line trenches where they halted and opened enfilade fire down them. Having inflicted many casualties, they drove my men out of the front line, who withdrew about 500 yards, the enemy remaining on the position they had captured.*

As the destruction of 2/W. Yorks had exposed the Londons' left and the tanks came on again, another retirement to the Cachy Switch followed.

Commanding 2/10 Londons, which had been allocated to 173 Brigade for counterattacks, Lieutenant Colonel William Symonds sought, on his own initiative, to regain the line north of Hangard Wood West but was mortally wounded while reconnoitring. Launched at 10 am, the 2/10th's counterattack went only 200 yards before fire from the wood halted it. The battalion pulled back to fill the gap between 2/4 and 2/2 Londons, giving 173 Brigade both the strength and the will to stand fast. Disheartened by heavy losses, the 77th Reserve, a poor quality formation, stopped well short of Cachy. As for the supporting tanks, *Elfriede* had strayed northward while pursuing 2/4 Londons and fallen into a quarry on the Hangard road at U.5.c.8.7, after which its crew surrendered. *Nixe, Siegfried and Shnuck* were fighting history's first tank-versus-tank battle.[8]

Tanks

Heneker knew at 7.20 am that the Germans were using tanks and Butler had been told by 8 am. Butler gave X Company's seven

Whippets in the Bois de Blangy to Major General Cator and Heneker handed over the three Mark IV's that the 8th Division held in the Bois l'Abbé to Brigadier General Grogan of 23 Brigade. He ordered Captain John Brown, the tanks' commander, to prevent the Germans reaching the Cachy Switch, the next line they would strike. Their crews dazed by gas, the tanks approached it at 9.30 am. Lieutenant Francis Mitchell's vehicle, No. 1 Tank of No. 1 Section of A Company, almost ran over the occupants:

> Suddenly, out of the ground 10 yards away, an infantryman rose, waving his rifle furiously. We stopped. He ran forward and shouted through the flap, 'Look out! Jerry tanks about!' . . . Opening the loophole, I looked out. There, some 300 yards away, a round, squat-looking monster was advancing. Behind it came waves of infantry and further away to left and right crawled two more of these armed-tortoises.

Mitchell was looking at *Nixe*, commanded by Lieutenant Wilhelm Biltz, which, like *Elfriede*, had veered northeast of Cachy. As he watched, its shells hit the two female Mark IV's in the section. Armed only with machine guns, they were powerless to reply and limped rearwards, badly holed. Mitchell's tank, a male with 6-pounders, fired twice but both shots missed. *Nixe* replied with a long burst of armour-piercing ammunition, filling No. 1's interior with sparks and flying splinters. Taking cover in the narrow re-entrant running down to the Bois d'Aquenne in U.4.a, No. 1 fired two more rounds but the tank 'was going up and down like a ship in a heavy sea' over the shellholes and they also missed. Then the Lewis gunner was wounded and yet another round went wide. Mitchell knew that stopping No. 1 was the only way of getting an accurate shot:

The end of *Elfriede*.

A Mark IV tank goes through its paces.

The pause was justified; a carefully aimed shot hit the turret of the German tank, bringing it to a standstill. Another roar and yet another white puff at the front of the tank denoted a second hit! Peering with swollen eyes through his narrow slit the elated gunner shouted words of triumph that were drowned by the roaring of the engine. Then once more with great deliberation he aimed and hit for the third time.

The first shell destroyed *Nixe's* gun and the next two struck the right side, whereupon the crew bailed out. When Biltz saw that the engines were still running, they reboarded and nursed the tank 2,000 yards rearward before it broke down altogether.

Scattering the infantry with case shot, Mitchell engaged *Siegfried and Shnuck*. They retired to let the artillery deal with his tank. Chased by shells and a bomber that appeared overhead, it was eventually knocked out by a salvo that blew off a track and damaged the engine. Mitchell and his crew escaped on foot as the Whippets raced into action.

Lieutenant Francis Mitchell.

A British pilot had dropped a message to the 58th Division stating that two German battalions were halted 1,000 yards southeast of Cachy. Captain Tommy Price, X Company's commander, received the news at 10.30 am. Price had won the DSO with 6/Northants at Boom Ravine in 1917 and his old comrades were delighted to see him in the current crisis. He got the Whippets started on the three-mile

Nixe **after the Germans stripped it of useful parts.**

drive to the northern side of Cachy, where he gave his orders. Forming a line at fifty-yard intervals, they were to charge at full-speed through the Germans to the Domart road, which Price pointed out on the skyline, turn about and charge back through them. He reported an astonishing success:

> *The charging tanks came upon* [the Germans] *over a rise, at point-blank range, apparently having a meal as several bodies had laid aside arms. The tanks went straight through them, causing great execution by fire, and by running over many who were unable to get away. They turned and came back through the remnants again, utterly dispersing them . . .*

Seeing the carnage, Lieutenant Bitter in *Siegfried* headed back to Cachy, rallied the infantry and met the Whippets 800 yards from the village as they were returning. Three were disabled – whether by *Siegfried* or the artillery is not known. A fourth had been destroyed when it strayed over the Domart road. Some accounts say the 77th

A Whippet light tank.

Reserve Division lost 400 men. *Siegfried* went back with *Schnuck* to the tank rendezvous.[9]

The British tanks were not finished yet. At 8.40 am Butler had sent the 8th Division two more, a male and a female, which Heneker intended to use in a counterattack by 1/Sherwood Foresters that was to retake the western end of Villers-Bretonneux. The Foresters had been recalled from Blangy-Tronville at 4 am, having arrived there at 2 am after their relief. At 11 am, Heneker added to the plan an attack by 25 Brigade, in which 2/R. Berks and two companies of 2/Rifle Brigade were to recapture the northern part of the town.

Moving along the southern side of the Bois d'Aquenne, the Foresters arrived at about 12.30 pm at the deep cut that crosses the Cachy Road and runs along the wood's eastern edge. As they turned northwards, 5 Guard Grenadier shot them up. The Foresters attacked but their commanding officer, Lieutenant Colonel Robert Moore, was badly wounded and the tanks, which were north of the wood, could not assist. Leaderless, they fell back to the D523, which separates the Bois d'Aquenne from the Bois l'Abbé. German shelling of the road caused severe losses as they dug in. 25 Brigade's counterattack was cancelled when Brigadier General Coffin pointed out that it would be suicidal in daylight and that, in any case, 2/Rifle Brigade did not have two companies left.

The order did not reach the tanks, which pressed on. The male tank was disabled by a field gun that the Germans had dragged to the edge of Villers-Bretonneux. Braving intense fire as it passed through the line formed by 2/E. Lancs and the Australians, the female destroyed several machine guns on the northwestern outskirts and cleared the tiny copse at O.28.b.5.2, behind the modern *gendarmerie*. Lieutenant Colonel Hill was then able to move the line onto higher ground. Its left rested on the copse, strengthening the junction with 2/R. Berks, and its right advanced 150 yards to O.28.d.0.5, the location Lieutenant Christian's patrol had occupied in the morning.

Though the Germans held the town and a pocket four miles wide and one deep around it that included the Bois d'Aquenne and Hangard Wood, they had been contained, and the British were strengthening the line ahead of them. 9 and 12/Londons from 175 Brigade had reinforced the 173rd, and 174 Brigade, which Cator sent forward from Cagny at 4 am, replaced the 175th in the Gentelles Line. In turn, Butler had given Cator 54 Brigade to replace the 174th as his divisional reserve. He deployed it forward, the rest of 6/Northants joining the two companies in the Cachy Switch, 7/Bedfords occupying it south of the village and

11/R. Fusiliers straddling today's D934, 1,000 yards southeast of Gentelles. On the opposite flank, Heneker had ordered 22/DLI to the Aubigny Line at 4.15 am. Looking on and straining to get involved were the Australians.

The Trials of the Australians

Brigadier General Elliott had issued his counterattack orders at 4.50 am. 59 Battalion was to assault up the high ground on which Villers-Bretonneux stood and 60 Battalion along the western spur of Hill 104 next to it. At the Hamelet Road, they were to turn southeast. The 60th would then advance to the Hamel road and the 59th would swing southwest to face the town on reaching the Roman Road. 57 Battalion was to be ready to move along the railway on the southern side of the town to cut the Germans off. Mobile fire support would come from Chestnut Troop, Royal Horse Artillery, which had been attached to 15 Brigade together with 4 Troop, 12 Australian Light Horse.

Fragmentary reports of a breakthrough from Lieutenant Christian and others were confirmed when 56 Battalion on Hill 104 stated at 8.35 am that Villers-Bretonneux had fallen and the Germans were attacking north from it. Elliott urged Hobbs to let him launch the counterattack. Hobbs allowed 15 Brigade to move to the start line, the D523, but said it could go no further unless the British actually asked for help. The battalions set off at 9.45 am. Angered by reports of unnecessary withdrawals by British soldiers, Elliott directed: 'All British troops to be rallied and reformed as our troops march through them by selected officers and on any hesitation to be shot'.

Hobbs at Bussy-les-Daours was as anxious as Elliott in Blangy-Tronville. At 8.59 am, shortly after telling Elliott that the counterattack was conditional on the British seeking his help, he offered Heneker 15 Brigade. Heneker's offhand attitude made Hobbs think that the offer was unwelcome. At 9.32 am he informed his corps commander, Lieutenant General Sir William Birdwood: 'We cannot get any information from 8th Div . . . we do not know whether they intend to counterattack'. In fact, Heneker had referred the offer to Butler, who declined it, saying that the 8th Division should be able to handle the situation. At 9.55 am, Hobbs told Elliott, 'British are endeavouring to restore the line. Our Division will stand fast until further orders'.

Elliott fumed. He knew the situation better than anyone because patrols from 4 Troop regularly reported to the Brigade Advanced Report Centre that the commander-designate of 58 Battalion, Lieutenant Colonel Charles Watson, was operating in a cowshed at the northern end of the Aubigny Line. Then Hobbs implicitly rebuked Elliott by ordering him to cancel the shooting stragglers order. Perhaps it was just as well because 59 and 60 Battalions had almost resorted to violence to stop a panicky battery firing into their rear and Elliott himself threatened to shoot some gunners haring across the Somme.[10]

Arguing Generals

Though neither Hobbs nor Elliott knew it, the loss of the town rocked the highest levels of the Allied command. When Rawlinson, who had staked his reputation on holding it, found out at 9.30 am, he ordered 13 Brigade, north of the Somme in Army Reserve, to march south 'to assist in [its] recapture, which was imperative for the security of Amiens'. Part of the 4th Australian Division, the formation was commanded by Brigadier General William Glasgow, a tough, taciturn Queensland Light Horseman. Like Elliott, he had foreseen what was coming and warned his battalions to be ready to move. They started their eight-mile march at 11.15 am, at which time 13 Brigade was put under Heneker. 49 Battalion would remain in reserve in the Aubigny Line, leaving 50, 51 and 52 Battalions for a counterattack. 55 Brigade, which had been recuperating west of Amiens, was also sent to III Corps.

Rawlinson's insistence that Villers-Bretonneux should be retaken before the Germans had a

Lieutenant Colonel Charles Watson.

Brigadier General William Glasgow.

chance to consolidate put Butler under pressure. At 10.50 am, he advised Heneker to bring 15 Brigade into the 8th Division's counterattacks. When Heneker replied that they were already underway, Butler urged Hobbs to co-operate as closely as possible with them. But Hobbs was still in the dark and the counterattacks had not started. Exasperated at the inactivity, Rawlinson told Butler at 11.30 am to have Heneker contact Hobbs with a view to counterattacking north and south of the town at 2 pm.

Heneker had already called off 25 Brigade's attack on the northern side of Villers-Bretonneux after Brigadier General Coffin argued that the Germans were so strongly established that a daylight advance without proper artillery preparation would amount to a massacre. Now ordered to mount a bigger attack under the same conditions, Heneker told Butler that it could not succeed and recommended instead a night attack by two brigades, ignoring the town itself but passing either side and meeting to the east of it. Around midday, he duly rang Hobbs, who again offered 15 Brigade or, because they were closer to the town, 14 Brigade's reserve battalions, the 55th and 56th. Awaiting Butler's answer, Heneker could only acknowledge the offer.

General Marie-Eugène Debeney.

Though Lieutenant Colonel Clement Armitage, Heneker's Chief of Staff, figured prominently, the exact authorship of the plan Heneker proposed is uncertain – as Bean says, it was 'a fairly common and obvious one for attacks on villages and small towns', and Elliott's own plan was similar. Both Rawlinson and

Butler approved it. The French, who had repulsed the Germans at Thennes but been driven back to the Bois de Sénécat south of the Avre, promised to co-operate if the attack were postponed until next day. Rawlinson's anger led General Debeney to order Major General Daugan's Moroccan Division to occupy the Gentelles Line up to the Bois l'Abbé that evening, thereby freeing some of the 58th Division's reserves. 'Debeney no good – cannot fight', Rawlinson wrote.

Hearing about the trouble when he called on Rawlinson at 12.30 pm, Haig had his representative on Foch's staff, Lieutenant General Sir John Du Cane, urge Foch to have the Moroccans join the counterattack. After lunching with Butler at Dury, Haig received a letter from Foch, in which he stated patronisingly that the importance of regaining Villers-Bretonneux would not have escaped Rawlinson, and pressed the British to counterattack as Debeney had done in the morning! Haig told Du Cane to inform Foch that Debeney had not attacked at all and to ask him again to have the Moroccans, or another French division, 'co-operate energetically and without delay' with III Corps, and then to relieve it as soon as possible. Though it was now too late for the French to contribute, Foch directed Debeney to assist more actively on 25 April and to look into the relief.[11]

Meanwhile, Glasgow had arrived at Glisy, where Heneker remarked that 13 Brigade would probably counterattack south of Villers-Bretonneux from the Bois de Blangy. As he had not seen the ground, Glasgow insisted on reconnoitring before the plan was finalised. Driving to the Bois de Blangy, he found Grogan and Brigadier General Roland Haig, the commander of 24 Brigade, exhausted at their headquarters under a railway bridge. A young staff officer assured him that there were troops ahead and that they would hold.

Rejoining Heneker at 2.30 pm, Glasgow said he would attack eastwards between the Bois l'Abbé and Cachy from a north-south line that the staff officer had indicated was clear of Germans. Heneker objected: 'But you can't do that. The corps commander says the attack is to be made from Cachy'. Glasgow refused. 'Why it's against all the teaching of your own army, Sir, to attack against the enemy's front. They'd get hell from the right'. The 77th Reserve Division on the Villers-Bretonneux-Domart road would enfilade that flank throughout the assault, whereas an easterly advance offered it some protection. 'Tell us what you want us to do, Sir, but you must let us do it our own way', he added, and Heneker conceded the point. Seeking surprise but also because many British guns were still settling into new positions after withdrawing, Glasgow ruled out a preliminary bombardment and

A barricade hastily erected in Villers-Bretonneux by its British defenders.

creeping barrage. Heneker concurred again.

When Glasgow foreshadowed an assault at 10.30 pm, Heneker ordered him to start at 8 pm and another flare-up ensued. Glasgow countered that it would still be light but Heneker replied that Butler wanted the attack done then. As Heneker had himself argued against a daytime attack, it is likely that he and Butler compromised with Rawlinson, who originally laid down a 2 pm start. Glasgow remonstrated: 'If it was God Almighty who gave the order, we couldn't do it in daylight. Here is your artillery largely out of action and the enemy with all his guns in position'. Through Heneker, Butler haggled with Glasgow, who also rejected 8.30, 9 and 9.30 pm before finally agreeing to attack at 10 pm.

Hobbs knew around 1 pm that 13 Brigade had been given to III Corps and must have realised that it was for a counterattack. Though nothing could be properly settled until Glasgow and Heneker completed their deliberations, he was not even told of the outline plan, which had been decided. Not until 3 pm did Butler inform him that the 5th Division had been placed under III Corps to assist a counterattack by the 8th, and only on calling Heneker at 3.30 pm did Hobbs ascertain that the 8th Division's role was to be carried out by 13 Brigade, which would be attacking south of the town to meet the 15th on the far side. The orders Elliott sent out at 4.15 pm were essentially those he had issued in the morning.

As Glasgow's conference with Heneker had just wrapped up then, its outcomes had yet to be felt, notably Glasgow's view that 13 Brigade was not strong enough to extend to the Roman Road. Heneker informed Hobbs, resulting in new orders from Elliott at 5.20 pm that confirmed 57 Battalion's enveloping drive along the railway but muddled its final objective by directing the 57th to stretch south to 13 Brigade after connecting with the 59th in 'our original front line' at P.25.c.0.3, close to the junction of the Roman and Hamel roads – the modern N29 roundabout site. The Hamel road had been the final objective in the orders Elliott had given since early morning but its junction with the Roman Road was almost a mile behind the 'original front line'.

The orders Butler issued at 5.30 pm clearly specified the old front line as the final objective and directed 15 Brigade to link with the 13th

Blangy-Tronville château, headquarters of both 13 and 15 Brigades.

in it 700 yards south of the Roman Road. Elliott summoned his battalion commanders to resolve any confusion, only to be told while explaining the final plan that, the Pioneer Battalion 22/DLI would be attached to 15 Brigade to mop up the northern part of Villers-Bretonneux. At 8 pm, Glasgow, who had earlier been given 2/Northants to mop up the southern part, arrived at Blangy-Tronville to share Elliott's headquarters. As the pair co-ordinated the inter-brigade arrangements, Glasgow saw that 57 Battalion could be caught up in the advance of the two British battalions. Elliott switched it to the northern side of the town. Fortunately, his battalion commanders were still present.[12]

Plan of Counterattack

Apart from the final objective, the tasks of 59 and 60 Battalions had not changed much. Leaving the D523 north of the railway on a 1,500-yard frontage, they would gain the Hamelet-Villers-Bretonneux road from the crossroads at O.18.b.6.3 to the town. Once there, the left of 60 Battalion was to swing forward until both battalions faced southeast for an advance to the old front line between 14 Brigade's right and the Roman Road. 57 Battalion would follow the right flank of the 59th, A and D Companies coming up on its right at the Hamelet road in order to extend to 13 Brigade, while B and C Companies faced the town, ready to clear its eastern end. Elliott arranged for 56 Battalion, which knew the ground, to supply 32 guides, one for each platoon of the 59th and 60th, and instructed Watson to move the advanced report centre to the western spur of Hill 104, where the headquarters of both battalions would be located.

Assembling on the Cachy end of the D523, 13 Brigade would advance through the switch to the old front line beyond Monument Wood, 51 Battalion on the left meeting the 57th and 52 Battalion on the right dropping companies off as the line bent around to the D23 crossroads at U.6.c.5.3. 50 Battalion following was to dig in 1,000 yards behind them. Like 22/DLI behind 15 Brigade, 2/Northants further back would head inwards as the advance passed Villers-Bretonneux to start the mopping up.

54 Brigade, organised as a composite formation comprising its own 7/Bedfords, 7/RW Kents from 53 Brigade, and 9/Londons from 175 Brigade of the 58th Division, was to regain the line from just west of the D23 crossroads to Hangard Wood. At 10 pm, the infantry step-off time, the artillery would lay a standing barrage on the town, the railway, Monument Wood and Hangard Wood East for an hour and then

110

put down a protective barrage 300 yards beyond the old British front line. When all formations were advised at 9.5 pm that Heneker was commanding the operation, 'Bimbo', the designated password, seemed singularly inappropriate. Nor did it convey any sense of the difficulties facing them, especially the Australian brigades that had the central role.[13]

Both were tired: 13 Brigade because it had forced marched all day and the 15th because it had been subjected to heavy gas shelling in the early morning and waited in suspenseful anticipation since. Both faced an assault of about 4,000 yards, during which 15 Brigade would have to change its axis, a complex business. The lateness of the orders meant rushed preparations at every level. 13 Brigade had not seen the ground but there was no time for reconnaissance. The Germans had been given a long time to get ready. On top of everything else, the attack was being made at night.

Sergeant Walter Downing of 57 Battalion thought there was not 'the remotest chance of success'. As the light faded on 24 April, Bean, too, was very pessimistic:

One cannot helping thinking of our magnificent 13th Bde going over – as they may be doing now. I don't believe they have a chance . . . I scarcely think it will come off, surely . . . Went to bed thoroughly depressed . . . feeling certain that this hurried attack would fail hopelessly.[14]

Whatever happened, though, the next day would be Anzac Day, and every Australian drew strength from the thought.

NOTES

1. F.S. Mason, *Memoir*, PP/MCR/231, IWM, pp. 85-92.
2. 'Narrative of Operations Carried Out by 8th Division 24-8 April 1918', 8 Div WD, Item 21/82, AWM 45.
3. Capt. Brodie, 'The First German Tank Attack At Villers-Bretonneux on 24 April 1918', in *Army Quarterly*, Vol. 19, No.2, January 1930, pp. 381-2.
4. D. Fletcher (ed.), *Tanks and Trenches* (Alan Sutton, 1994), p. 112; 2/M'sex WD, 24 April 1918, WO 95/173, TNA.
5. WD entries for 24 April 1918: 2/W. Yorks, WO 95/174; 2/Devons, WO 95/1712; 23 Bde, 95/1711; all TNA.
6. 2/Rifle Bde and 2/R. Berks WD, 24 April 1918, WO 95/1731 and 95/1279, TNA.
7. 2/E. Lancs WD, 24 April 1918, WO 95/1729, TNA; *OH*, p. 546.
8. WD entries for 24 April 1918: 2/2, 2/4 Londons, WO 95/3001; 2/10 Londons, WO 95/3009; all TNA; 58 Div, Item 21/A, AWM 45.
9. Mitchell in P. Slowe and R. Woods, *Fields of Death*, (Robert Hale, 1986), pp. 180-3; Fletcher, op. cit., pp. 105, 115-6; B.H. Liddell Hart, *The Tanks*, I (Cassell, 1959), pp. 167-8.

10. In/Out Messages, 24-6 April 1918, 15 Bde WD, Item 23/15, Roll 29, AWM 4; 5 Div WD, 24 April 1918, Item, Roll, AWM 4.

11. *Military Operations II*, p. 394; OH, p. 570; Simkins, 'For Better or Worse', p. 25.

12. *OH*, pp. 574-5; SG 16/12 and BM 410, 24 April 1918, 15 Bde WD.

13. III Corps G596, 5.30 pm, 24 April, 1918, WD; WO 95/678, TNA; 8 Div Order 287, 24 April 1918, WD, Item 21/82, AWM 45.

14. W.H. Downing, *To The Last Ridge* (Duffy & Snellgrove, 1998), p. 125; Bean D112, 24 April 1918, Item 108, 3DRL 606/18, AWM 38.

Chapter Seven

VILLERS-BRETONNEUX REGAINED

The evening of 24 April was fine apart from a brief shower at 8 pm, and clouds covered the moon. But the shelling of Villers-Bretonneux, which was still smouldering from the morning bombardment, started more fires, one large building towards the northern side becoming an inferno, and the flames served as a beacon for the advancing brigades.

13 Brigade
Captain Hubert Essame, adjutant of 2/Northants, was much impressed by the calmness of the Australian officers assembled in the twilight at the Northants' headquarters in the Bois de Blangy, where their battalion commanders and his own commanding officer, Lieutenant Colonel Stephen Latham, were giving orders. The company commanders had only ten minutes to brief the platoon commanders, so the men got their orders as they moved up along the wood's southern rim. Because Monument Wood had to be reached before the barrage lifted from it at 11 pm, the leading wave was told to press on regardless, leaving the follow-up wave to mop up. Leading A Company, 51 Battalion, Captain Billy Harburn drummed the point home: 'The Monument is your goal and nothing is to stop your getting there. Kill every bloody German you see, we don't want any prisoners, and God bless you'.

The action had already begun for the intelligence officers taping out the start line. It was supposed to run from the southernmost tip of the Bois d'Aquenne, which 1/Sherwood Foresters were assumed to be holding. I/5 Guard Grenadier and 3 Machine Gun Company were the actual occupants and they opened fire, forcing the tape to be laid 300 yards rearward. 52 Battalion shook out along it at 9.45 pm. Fully alert, the Germans in the Bois d'Aquenne sent up a flare that enabled a machine gun to engage the 51st as it arrived at 9.53 pm. The barrage lit the skyline at 10 pm, revealing Monument Farm at the end of a long, leisurely incline. The counter-barrage opened at 10.05 pm and struck the two battalions. Their assembly complete, they were relieved to step off five minutes later.

No sooner had the advance begun than flares shot up like roman candles from the Bois d'Aquenne, and 3 Machine Gun Company's gunners saw A Company in enfilade to them as it moved on the left of

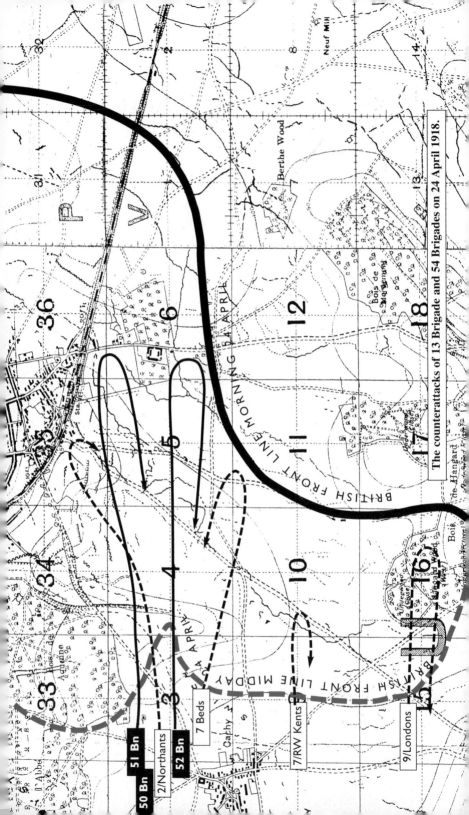

The counterattacks of 13 Brigade and 54 Brigades on 24 April 1918.

51 Battalion. A torrent of fire lashed Harburn's men as they lay motionless under the dazzling light. Lieutenant Clifford Sadlier commanded the flank platoon:

We wondered what had struck us. Before we had gone 50 yards, 39 out of the 42 in my platoon were in the mud either dead or wounded. I hit the deck and saw that Charlie Stokes from another platoon was still alive and 2 bombers . . . had also escaped the fire. I knew that if we did not clean out the edge of that wood, the 51st Battalion would be sitting ducks.

Sadlier asked B Company in support to replace his platoon in the advance and told Stokes, sergeant of the adjacent platoon, to collect his bombers for an attack on the wood.

Stokes found six which, with Sadlier's pair, made nine men altogether. Sadlier won the Victoria Cross for leading them in a crazy rush against not just the machine guns and I/5 Guard Grenadier but also the first elements of I and II/5 Foot Guards arriving to relieve it. His citation reads:

Although himself wounded, he... succeeded in killing the crews and capturing two of the guns. By this time Lieutenant Sadlier's party were all casualties, and he alone attacked a third enemy machine-gun with his revolver, killing the crew of four and taking the gun. In doing so he was again wounded. The very gallant conduct of this officer was the means of clearing the flank, and

The left flank of 51st Battalion and Lieutenant Sadlier's charge.

Lieutenant Clifford Sadlier.

Bois d'Aquennes

Monument Farm

Lancer Wood

Hangard Wood

German machine guns

Lieutenant Sadlier

51Bn

allowing the battalion to move forward, thereby saving a most
critical situation.

It does not say that Sadlier was shot point blank in the thigh at the outset by a German shouting *'Kamerad'*, whom he then killed, or that the second wound paralysed his arm. With only two men left, Stokes took over and knocked out another three machine guns, using captured German bombs when his own ran out. He was also recommended for the VC but higher authority, in an act of bureaucratic idiocy, decided that only one should be given for the action and he received the DCM instead. His citation differs little from that for Sadlier's VC.

As the rest of the line advanced under relatively harmless long-range fire, a flurry of shots rang out in front. 'Bomb the bastards', someone yelled, and grenades were thrown. The subsequent rush found some 2/Devons and 1/Worcs in the Cachy Switch. Unaware of the counterattack, they had thought the Germans were behind them. As the line passed over the switch and approached the wire protecting it, the fire became intense. Several machine guns were on the far side but the deadliest fired along the wire from a sunken road that crossed the Cachy road at the edge of the Bois d'Aquenne. This location was in the narrow re-entrant that ran down to the wood, the sides of which made a perfect fire lane for the machine gunner, who had the line in enfilade until Sergeant Stokes silenced him. 'Next day', says Bean, 'the wire was lined with the dead of the two battalions'.

The machine guns up ahead belonged to III/5 Guard Grenadier and the 77th Reserve Division, and were dotted in shell holes and bits of trench between the switch and the Domart road. Company Sergeant Major Elfeldt saw five of them firing at 52 Battalion, which had arrived just as a field kitchen on the road was preparing to feed 7 Company, II/5 Foot Guards:

> *The leading men fall but others charge on. These too are*
> *mown down, but new waves always come on cheering in their*
> *place and rush forward into our machine-gun fire... As the line*
> *gives way, the English machine-gun fire strikes it from front and*
> *flank. The English follow hard on our heels. With great uproar*
> *they sweep through the dark night. Where at some points an*
> *attempt is made to put them on their defence, their machine-gun*
> *fire soon breaks down the resistance, and mows down many of*
> *our troops.*

51 Battalion had become disorganised at the wire and was continuing in small groups. Some of them came across 6 Company, II/5 Foot Guards, which was also at its field kitchen on the Domart road.

Lieutenant Krüger led his men in a charge that gained some ground before the Australians routed them in a wild mêlée. When other Germans surrendered on the left, Captain Harburn bellowed 'No prisoners', later remarking that he did not know what to do with them. He had just managed to gather forty men of A Company when about 200 men from I and II/5 Foot Guards charged, firing from the hip. The left company of 50 Battalion, which Harburn had called forward because his own force was so weak, fortuitously arrived and the Germans fled towards Villers-Bretonneux. Few got away.

A Company was now above the hollow on the southern side of the town. Machine guns fired from the railway embankment on the far side, which was like a rampart at the town limit then but is largely hidden by urban sprawl today. Seeing Monument Wood 1000 yards eastwards, Harburn ignored them. During the advance towards it, Lance Corporal Cec Burt and Privates Reg Helyar and Bertie Denman became disoriented and blundered into a strongpoint manned by forty Germans in the hollow. Helyar grenaded it and Burt threatened the Germans with his damaged Lewis gun, which could only fire single shots. They surrendered nonetheless, whereupon the eigthteen-year old Denman shouted, 'What shall we do with them? Shoot them? Stick them?' Helyar brusquely replied: 'For God's sake shut up. Cec's gun is useless and my bombs are napoo. This crowd could eat us if they liked.' The Germans were led rearwards.

The rest of A Company reached the D23 between the railway and Monument Farm, where Harburn left them to find whomever was on his right. Other groups from 51 Battalion were also making for Monument Wood, one coming across *Elfriede* lying on its side in the quarry on the Hangard road. Still others had become mixed up with the left of 52 Battalion, part of which entered the farm orchard. Like

Monument Farm from the hollow on the southern side of Villers-Bretonneux. 2/Northants tried to attack the town from this vicinity. 36 Battalion's charge on 4 April began from the far end.

Monument Farm

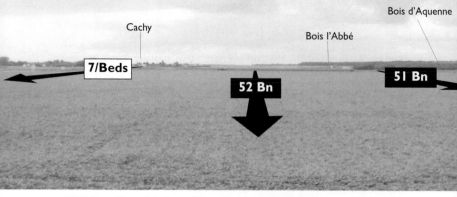

III/5 Foot Guards' view of the advance of 13 Brigade and 7/Bedfords.

Harburn's men, they had been able to approach unnoticed because III/5 Foot Guards were dug in along the D23 on the other side of the farm and dealing with an attack by the bulk of the 52nd's left.

The Foot Guards had run out of flares and could not tell whether the men in front were friendly. A few flares finally appeared and were fired, unveiling 'a dense crowd of khaki uniforms and plate helmets'. Against a devastating fusillade from the German machine guns, the assault could make no headway. The rest of 52 Battalion had veered southeast towards more machine guns that were holding up neighbouring 7/Bedfords on the Hangard road. Major William Craies had a platoon fill the resulting gap and sought to tie in the 52nd's flank with the Bedfords, whom he found entrenching 200 yards east of the road in U.11.a. They had reached the old support line but thought they were on their objective, the old front line, which was actually 300 yards further east. Heavily shelled at this stage, they withdrew beyond the Domart Road.

Faced with a fragile flank on the left, stiff resistance on the D23 and the Bedfords' retirement on the right, Craies realised that 52 Battalion could not continue. Leaving outposts along the Hangard road, he drew its line back to the Domart road where it connected with the Bedfords. Harburn turned up and was told that the line could not extend to his location half a mile to the northeast. At 1 am he ordered his men to fall back onto the left of 52 Battalion, which put that end of the line 500 yards from the railway across the hollow. The other advanced groups gradually came in and sixteen machine guns were set up on the new perimeter.[1]

15 Brigade

Elliott's late afternoon conference with his battalion commanders made the timings in 15 Brigade extremely tight. Already forward in the Aubigny Line, 57 Battalion was less affected but 59 and 60 Battalions on the Somme flats near Blangy-Tronville were almost two miles from the start line on the D523. The 60th got underway at 9.10 pm and, helped by the guides positioned along the approach routes, arrived close to zero hour. 59 Battalion left at 8.30 pm and did not. A guide had warned Captain Fred Bursey, leading C Company, to avoid a dip in which gas lingered and it got lost detouring in the dark. As C Company was supposed to be on the left of the 59th and next to the 60th, the two battalions were not in touch when the attack should have started. A Company under Captain Eric Young had arrived on the right but B and D Companies were still on their way.

Lieutenant Colonel Norman Marshall, 60 Battalion's commander, checked the start line at 10.15 pm while going to the headquarters on Hill 104, and found the 60th waiting for the 59th. He directed that the advance must not begin without his approval and despatched officers to locate the errant companies. B Company, in the 59th's second wave, appeared soon afterwards and Marshall told its commander, Captain George Smith, to take C Company's place. Led by Captain Bob Morgan, D Company, the first from 57 Battalion to arrive, would support him if the other companies did not show up. D Company of the 59th duly appeared. Shortly before midnight, almost two hours too late to take advantage of the barrage and with Bursey's company still lost, Marshall waved them off.

Wearing white armbands for easy identification, the Australians started up the slope ahead of the D523. 59 Battalion passed through scattered parties of 2/R. Berks but the rest saw no friendly troops. Emerging from the hollow on the northern side of Villers-

Lieutenant Colonel Norman Marshall.

15 Brigade's advance as seen from the southern end of its start line on the D523.

Start Line

Aust National Memorial (Hill 104)

15 Brigade

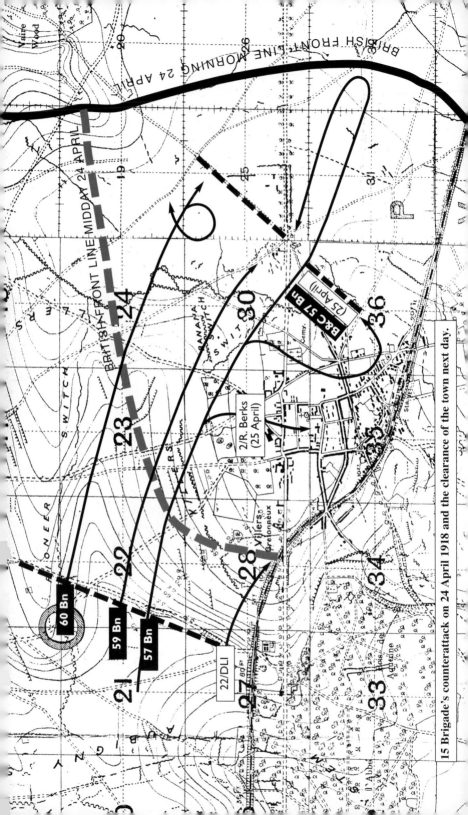

BRITISH FRONT LINE MORNING 24 APRIL

BRITISH FRONT LINE MIDDAY 24 APRIL

Vaire Wood

P

B&G 57 BN (25 April)

2/R. Berks (25 April)

SWITCH

BANANA SWITCH

PIONEER SWITCH

SWITCH

Villers Bretonneux

60 Bn

59 Bn

57 Bn

22/DLI

Achenne

15 Brigade's counterattack on 24 April 1918 and the clearance of the town next day.

Lamotte-Warfuseé

Charge starts from the Hamelet Road

Villers-Bretonneux

HAMELET ROAD (1ST OBJECTIVE)

60 Bn

59 & 57 Bns

15 Brigade's attack as seen from Hill 104. The charge began from the Hamelet road, after which the drift towards the town became pronounced.

Bretonneux, where the counter-barrage petered out, they started crabbing towards the burning town. Luckily, the flames were behind the Germans, who could see nothing in the blackness. At 12.40 am, having come a mile unopposed, the advance reached the first objective, the Hamelet road, and paused while the leaders organised the rightwards pivot to face southeast. C Company finally caught up and assumed its position.

A and D Companies, 57 Battalion were moving onto the right of A Company, 59 Battalion when the scouts forming a protective screen ahead reported movement nearby. Young, who had been wounded in the shelling, accordingly shifted the right flank towards the orchard in O.29.b on the northern edge of the town. The adjustment was detected. Two flares went up and a machine gun fired erratically. 'In a calm, easy voice', a sergeant recalled, Young gave the order to charge. Releasing their pent-up tension, the Australians unleashed a banshee yell, 'sufficient to make the enemy's blood run cold', Lieutenant Colonel John Scanlan of the 59th said, as they sprang forward like a horde of Viking berserkers. 13 Brigade heard the ferocious cry while fighting over a mile away.

'For the time being' wrote Bean, 'the men had thrown off the restraints of civilised intercourse and were what the bayonet instructors of all armies aimed at producing – primitive, savage men.' 15 Brigade had perfected what Elliott called 'the throat jab', a

Lieutenant Colonel John Scanlan.

121

thrust 'under the chin and upwards into the spinal cord', that was 'most difficult to parry... Struck thus a man dies easily, quickly and painlessly, often without a cry or a movement. Our men practice it assiduously and in a mêlée it makes them invincible.' The 5th Division's history records:

> A storm of enemy machine gun and rifle fire was poured into the oncoming ranks but checked them not at all. A hundred enemy flares lit the terrible scene in vivid light, in which the Germans read too well their fate. Shriek following shriek marked the toll of the deadly bayonets and good round Australian oaths were ripped out in quick succession as the panting men plunged forward to the next victims. The German defences were arranged in a series of strong posts distributed in depth... if for a moment the slaughter slackened, it was because new victims were wanted and, in the dark, they were not easy to see. But soon the enemy flares would shoot up again from strong points not yet reached. Those flares were the death warrant of many a German that night, for, guided by them, the assailants knew exactly where their enemies lay.[2]

The right of the attack passed through a belt of old British wire as though it did not exist. 'The Boche screamed for mercy', Sergeant Roy Fynch of 59 Battalion remarked, 'but there were too many machine guns about to show them any consideration as we were moving forward'. Sergeant Walter Downing of the 57th almost pitied the Germans:

> They had no chance in the wild onslaught of maddened men... They killed and killed. Bayonets passed with ease through grey-clad bodies, and were withdrawn with a sucking sound... One huge Australian advanced firing a Lewis Gun from the shoulder, spraying the ground with lead... One saw running forms in the dark, and the flashes of rifles, then the evil pyre in the town flared and showed to their killers the white faces of Germans lurking in shell holes, or flinging away their arms and trying to escape, only to be stabbed or shot down as they ran . . . It was impossible to take prisoners. Men could not be spared to take them to the rear; also they might easily have conducted them, in the deceiving light, to the enemy lines behind us.

The charge had smashed through 478 IR, and annihilated a company of II/35 Fusilier north of the orchard. A machine gun concealed by a haystack there proved especially troublesome. Shot through both legs, Lieutenant Alison O'Brien of 59 Battalion called out, 'Carry on boys,

German machine gunners killed at the start of 15 Brigade's charge.

I'm hit'. Sergeant Naylor led the platoon towards a German officer and his men, whose hands were up. As Naylor approached, the officer dropped his hands and shot him, with predictable results. Naylor was badly wounded; the German was killed. But later, says Bean, 'as the men tired of the killing, prisoners came back by droves'. Fired on near the junction of the Hamel and Roman Roads, for example, Corporal Arthur Rusden and four men bombed some Germans and demanded their surrender. A voice answered in perfect English, 'No, you will only shoot us if we come out'.

> *'No', replied one of our chaps, 'You are prisoners'. As soon as the word prisoners passed his lips there was a clatter of rifles and equipment as it was thrown off and out filed 20 Huns, all very meek and docile and seemingly quite pleased with their fate.*

By 2 am, the assault had gone beyond the Hamel road but all three battalions were hopelessly intermixed. The order to halt was given and they reformed on the line of the road, which 59 and 60 Battalions and their guides from the 56th said was the final objective. Captain Morgan of the 57th insisted it had not been reached. They were all correct because the old British front line crossed the Hamel road on the left of 60 Battalion's sector then headed due south to cross the Roman Road on the far side of the airfields, 1,300 yards from the 57th on the right. The confusion, which stemmed from the late changes to the orders Elliott issued on 24 April, should have been resolved at his final

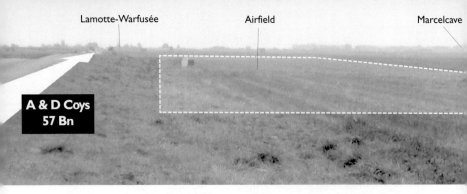

A & D Coys
57 Bn

15 Brigade's right flank on the Roman Road. The objective here, the old front line, actually crossed 1,300 yards closer to misty Lamotte-Warfusée.

conference. No senior officers were present to resolve it now.

Morgan led his company and A Company, 57 Battalion through the airfields, where they captured many Germans in the hangars. Reaching the old front line at P.26.c.5.3, they stretched south towards the railway. After fifteen minutes, during which there was no sign of 13 Brigade on the right and the Germans were seen moving around the left, they headed back to the Hamel/Roman Road junction and, overlapping the right flank of 59 Battalion, bent back along the Roman Road towards the town. B and C Companies of 57 Battalion had carried out their difficult orders to the letter during the advance, wheeling in a semi-circle to face the town and protect the rear of the final assault. Their line ran northwest from the Roman Road to the orchard in O.29.b from whence the fight had begun.

60 Battalion's drift towards the heavier resistance on the town side frustrated the efforts of D Company on the left, under Lieutenant John Simpson, to find the flank of 14 Brigade. On reaching the Hamel road, Simpson's left rested on the crossroads at P.25.b.2.8, 700 yards from the 14th's right, and his patrols ran into the Germans while looking for it. He swung his company back to form a flank 600 yards long facing northeast. Taking out a patrol himself, Simpson captured twenty Germans and four machine guns but 14 Brigade remained elusive. Marshall arrived at dawn and ordered another patrol out. Again led by Simpson, it ran into a post that surrendered but then fire from a second post wounded all but Simpson and his sergeant. When the Germans who capitulated became aggressive, he killed them and dragged the wounded into their post, where they remained, pinned down by the other post, until nightfall. As the Germans were clearly dug in between the two brigades, the gap remained.

At 3.20 am Elliott sent 58 Battalion up from the Aubigny Line with instructions to exploit towards Warfusée if the opportunity arose or reinforce the forward battalions if a counterattack developed. As in 13

Brigade, their positions bristled with machine guns, seventeen in all, eight of which were captured. Though neither brigade had retaken the old British front line, they had between them nearly encircled Villers-Bretonneux and regained most of the ground lost on the northern part of the battlefield.[3]

54 Brigade

Made up of battalions brought together from other brigades shortly before the counterattack, 54 Brigade lacked the slickness of the Australian brigades, whose battalions were used to fighting alongside each other. Its assault, which had to cover 1,800 yards against the 77th Reserve Division, enjoyed mixed fortunes.

Extended across a 1,000-yard frontage between U.15.b.0.5 and U.21.b.0.5, 9/Londons on the right were to recapture Hangard Wood West. Their orders did not arrive until 8.30 pm but the Londons were already close to their start line and all but D Company left on time. A and B Companies reached their objective, the Hangard road on the far side of the wood, but could not hold it and withdrew. At no stage did they see 7/RW Kents on their left, who had formed up parallel to the D523 south of Cachy and stepped off at 10.05 pm. Swept by machine guns in shell-hole posts, they lost over 230 men in the next hour. The survivors dug in west of the Domart road, half way to the old British front line. B Company on the left had suffered the heaviest casualties and lost touch with 7/Bedfords, who were attacking next to 13 Brigade.

The Bedfords encountered only slight resistance for the first thousand yards but when they crossed the Hangard road, some of the machine guns that had stopped 7/RW Kents also held them. They began digging in on what was assumed to be old front line, which they were to occupy south of U.5.d.9.2, but was, in fact, the support line a few hundred yards short of it. Shelled on linking up with 52 Battalion, the Bedfords fell back to a line 200 yards west of the Domart road. Germans who had not been mopped up were in the surrounding shell holes, preventing contact with 7/RW Kents. By early morning, only 2/Lieutenant W. Tysoe and 160 men were left to hold a line 800 yards long.[4]

The Fight for the Town and the Bois d'Aquenne

Closer to Villers-Bretonneux, 2/Northants had just stepped off behind 51 Battalion when the counter-barrage plastered its headquarters, killing Lieutenant Colonel Latham, wounding Captain Essame and temporarily halting its advance. The Northants caught up at the Cachy

Switch wire, where the machine gun feasting on the 51st cut them up as well until Sergeant Stokes destroyed it. Lieutenant Mason recalled:

> *There seemed to be machine guns all around and we went through a devilish crossfire. We began to fall over dead Australians, and then topping a small ridge, we saw Villers-Bretonneux, its church burning like a torch. The advance was halted and we were waiting and watching the burning church, its red glow illuminating the field sloping away from our ridge. There were many black blobs which were not shell holes. They were obviously deceased Aussies.*

Commanded now by Major H.T. Forster, the Northants turned northeast for the assault on the town. As they descended the hollow towards it, flares turned the little re-entrant into a well-lit amphitheatre for the machine guns on the railway. Casualties were again heavy and Forster led his men to the high ground further east for another try. Progress proving impossible, they formed a defensive flank facing north that connected with Captain Harburn's left.

As for 22/DLI, Elliott was unable to locate its commander, Lieutenant Colonel R.C. James, until 9 pm. Arriving at Blangy-Tronville at 9.30 pm seemingly unaware that his battalion was to clear the northern half of Villers-

Lieutenant Colonel Stephen Latham. *(Northamptonshire Regiment Museum, Abington Museum, Northampton).*

Bretonneux, James continually complained about the lack of time, peeving Elliott who 'impressed upon him that providing he mopped up the village during the night it really did not matter what time he moved'. Starting even later than 15 Brigade, 22/DLI encountered heavy fire from the northwestern outskirts and did not press its attack. At 3.30 am, Elliott received a message from Lieutenant Colonel Herbert Layh, the commander of 57 Battalion, behind which the Durhams should have been, saying there was no sign of them.

When Heneker called Elliott at 4.15 am on 25 April to inquire about 22/DLI's progress, he replied that he had no news but, judging by James' earlier pessimism and indecisiveness, they had probably not moved at all. Heneker ordered Brigadier General Coffin to have 2/R. Berks start the mopping up in their place. As machine gun and sniper fire from the northeastern outskirts was greatly hampering 15 Brigade's reorganization, Layh had already recommended to Elliott that the contingency plan for the 57th to do it should go ahead. At 6 am, B and C Companies swept down the 600-yard wide corridor formed by the Hamelet road and the track through O.30 central. After moving through the eastern half of the town, they were to wheel left to a line running south of the Roman Road in order to link up with 13 Brigade.

Led by Captain Les Elliott, B Company on the right met 2/R. Berks, who had advanced through the orchards 300 yards west, at the Fouilloy-Hamelet crossroads. They pushed on together, the Lewis gunners spraying the front of any building from which fire came, the

Edition Colmaire

(Above) **Looking northeast from Villers-Bretonneux along the Hamelet road.**

(Left) **The same view today.**

bombers grenading the back, whereupon the occupants usually surrendered. Sixty were captured around the intersection of the Roman and Fouilloy Roads, 150 by the time the town square area was reached. C Company on the left took just as many. As neither company could spare men to escort them, the prisoners were handed over to the Berks and to 22/DLI, which had finally managed to break into the town.

At 10.30 am, B Company had reformed, wheeled left and was just starting off again when firing broke out behind it. Turning back, Lieutenant David Falconer's platoon took a prisoner who revealed that a big group of Germans was holed up by the railway station. Part of the platoon was about to assault it when more firing erupted from the D23 bridge, 165 yards along the track. Falconer saw six of his men there shooting at large numbers of Germans withdrawing eastwards between the southern bank of the railway cutting and Monument Farm.

Unlike 207 RIR at the far end of the town, Captain Teichmann, who commanded II/48 IR towards the eastern end, had realised early on that he was almost cut off. His initial reaction was to stay put and urge the 228th Division to counterattack westwards along the Roman Road as soon as possible. The only unit readily available, III/35 Fusilier, did so at 7.20 am but stood no chance. 207 RIR and I/48 IR were now pulling

The German escape route along the railway towards Monument Farm.

Monument Wood

Villers-Bretonneux railway station after the battle.

out and, with fighting going on in the streets around his headquarters, Teichmann did the same. II/35 Fusilier left at 8.30 am. The Germans mostly headed for the station, beyond which lay the safety of the 4th Guards Division's flank at Monument Wood.

The Bois d'Aquenne garrison was already through. At 4 am Heneker had ordered the remnants of 23 Brigade, 440 men collected in the Gentelles Line in the Bois l'Abbé, to fill the gap between the Cachy Switch and the right of 25 Brigade north of the Roman Road. Starting on the Roman Road after first light, they had gone almost 1,000 yards before fire from the railway and the northern side of the Bois d'Aquenne halted them. 2/W. Yorks moved around to enter the wood from the southern side, where Captain S. Houlton, leading a section of three tanks, had just reported to Lieutenant Colonel Robert Christie, the commander of 51 Battalion, in the Cachy Switch. As machine guns

**Lieutenant Colonel
Robert Christie.**

were firing into the back of 13 Brigade's line from the wood, Christie told him to clear it.

While the tanks rolled down the rides, 2/W.Yorks worked northwards through the timber. At about 7 am, the Germans began running from the tree line towards Villers-Bretonneux and were engaged by 2/Middlesex from the road and the two companies of 2/Devons still in the Cachy Switch. Some surrendered when the tanks broke out and caught them in the hollow between the wood and the town. They were taken to the prisoner of war cage set up at the railway bridge on the D523. By 9.30 am, the Bois d'Aquenne was clear and 23 Brigade had established a thinly manned line in front of it. From the high ground above the hollow, 2/Northants shot up 5/Foot Guards racing eastwards on the far side. 93 RIR headed for the railway cutting below the Roman Road. The morning mist enabled most of these men to escape.

Without knowing it, Falconer's men on the bridge commanded the only line of withdrawal for those following. He asked Captain Elliott for reinforcements but the message went astray. A message from Elliott, ordering him back to the eastern outskirts to take up the new line, did not. Telling Falconer that the British would finish the mopping up, Elliott left two platoons, including Falconer's, in houses and trenches between the modern Rue de Montdidier and the Rue du 8 Mai facing southeast to guard against any attack from the bridge. The remainder of B and C Companies dug in a few hundred yards ahead of them from O.36.a.8.5. on the Rue du 8 Mai to O.30.d.5.3 on the Roman Road, an area that was mainly open fields then. 2/R. Berks withdrew to their old line north of Villers-Bretonneux and 22/DLI continued clearing the southeastern end of the town. 13 Brigade was nowhere to be seen.[5]

Doubt and Disbelief

Aware that the 4th Guard Division had been rolled back to the southern edge of Villers-Bretonneux, XIV Corps gave them its reserve, 74 IR, plus two battalions of 1 Grenadier for a joint counterattack with the 77th Reserve Division at 6 am. At 5.20 am, though, the 228th Division reported that the line north of the town had also gone. More bad news arrived when 74 IR and the Grenadiers said they could not be in position on time, and the counterattack had to be postponed to 8 am. They did not arrive behind the headquarters of 5 Foot Guards, near the D23 crossroads south of Monument Farm and close to the start position, until 9 am. By then the mist had lifted and the British artillery pounded them. The counterattack was cancelled and the troops used to strengthen the line. 78 and 91 IR, which XI Corps had sent from the 19th Division, relieved the 77th Reserve north of Hangard Wood.

For 13 Brigade and 54 Brigades, therefore, the morning seemed quiet, although it was not without incident for two Germans, one carrying a white handkerchief, had entered 7/Bedfords' line at 8 am. 2/Lieutenant Tysoe told CSM Burles to take them blindfolded to battalion headquarters but Burles was wounded on the way and they wandered into Lieutenant Mason's platoon of 2/Northants. In flawless English, the senior German introduced himself as a sergeant-major in the Prussian Guard – in fact, he was CSM Brückner of 332 IR, 77th Reserve Division – said he had lived at Muswell Hill and then came to the point:

> *My commander has sent me out with a verbal message. I seek a parlementaire with your commander. You are surrounded by three divisions of Prussian Guards and umpteen battalions of heavy guns and to avoid further bloodshed my commander wishes you to surrender.*

Mason took the pair to Major Forster, whom he found with Christie and Lieutenant Colonel John Whitham, the commander of 52 Battalion, at the Australian headquarters in the Cachy Switch. They had seen men digging in west of the Domart road behind the area thought to be occupied by 7/RW Kents, and asked Glasgow to check their identity with 54 Brigade. On receiving the surrender message, they realised that the diggers were German and that a counterattack was probably impending. While Mason escorted the two Germans to 24 Brigade's headquarters, another one arrived with a message from Captain von Linsingen, the commander of II/419 IR, 77th Reserve Division, demanding a meeting 'at once' with 'the officer

Lieutenant Colonel John Whitham.

who commands the troups [sic] there'. 'Tell them to go to Hell', Glasgow replied.

By now the mysterious entrenchers had set up machine guns and were sniping but the staffs of 54 Brigade and the 58th Division refused to believe that the Germans were west of the Domart road. At 5.35 pm, three Whippets, which Major General Cator had ordered to clear up the confusion, rolled out of Cachy and Whitham pointed them out. In a fifteen-minute onslaught, the tanks cleared the Germans from a crowded trench on the right of 7/RW Kents and west of Hangard Wood. Tysoe's men were discovered in isolated parties 200 yards *west* of the Domart road and the Germans *on the same side* 100 yards beyond them. There was no sign of British positions east of the road. Nonetheless, the British commanders still insisted that their line was there.

At 7 pm the Germans began an hour-long bombardment but no attack followed, apart from a sortie that penetrated the right of 7/Bedfords, where the gap with 7/RW Kents lay. Tysoe, who had refused another call to surrender, led a bayonet charge that ejected them. He received the DSO for his inspirational leadership. Reports of the Germans massing throughout the day had kept the British guns busy and the German artillery responded appropriately, killing Major Craies and Captain Morgan among others. In the end, the evening foray and III/35 Fusiliers' local effort in the morning represented the sum total of the German counterattack.[6]

The Door Closes

Notwithstanding the confusion on his right flank, Glasgow was always more concerned about his left, which lay nowhere near 15 Brigade even after 57 Battalion stretched south of the Roman Road. At 10 am, while the 57th was embroiled in the town, he had given the job of filling the gap to 50 Battalion, commanded by Lieutenant Colonel Alfred Salisbury. 2/Northants were to establish a support line through the station, 750 yards northeast of their line above the hollow. As the 50th was in depth in the Cachy Switch several hundred yards behind the Northants, it would be exposed to 5 Foot Guard's machine guns in Monument Farm and Wood for much longer. Even lone runners had trouble getting through. Salisbury wanted to wait until dark.

Major Forster attempted the Northants' part immediately. On his signal, they crossed the 150 yards to the shelter of the hollow in a headlong rush. 'It was about ¼ minute,' their War Diary says 'before the enemy grasped what was happening and opened very heavy fire

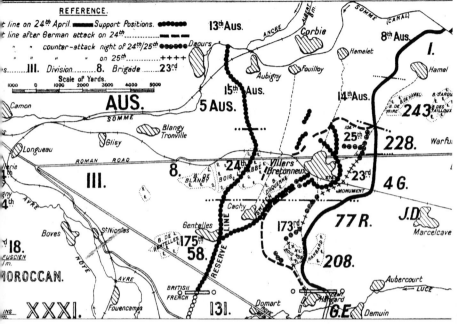

The seesawing battle on 24/25 April 1918.

and only the men who were slow suffered, about twelve casualties in all'. Forster established his headquarters under the railway bridge on the Cachy road and the companies headed for the station, mopped up some Germans north of it, and edged back across the hollow to connect with 51 Battalion. 22/DLI was at the southeastern corner of the town, where a German pocket still held out near the D23 bridge. Heneker offered Elliott four tanks to help eliminate it but he only took one. The other three went to Glasgow, who wanted them to clear Monument Wood and then assist 50 Battalion's night link-up.

Glasgow's tanks did not arrive and Elliott's conked out. Doing without them, a patrol from 50 Battalion worked across the lip of the hollow from 51 Battalion to meet a second patrol that had mopped up some Germans on the railway a few hundred yards beyond the D23 bridge. The 50th occupied the line gained, closing the gap south of the railway. Moving through the town, two companies of 49 Battalion, which had come up from the Aubigny Line, were guided into position between the railway and the right flank of 57 Battalion at 1 am on 26

133

April, closing the gap north of it. The line around Villers-Bretonneux was complete. Prodded by Foch, the French under Debeney were about to make their appearance on its continuation past Cachy.[7]

The French Connection

On 25 April, Rawlinson, Butler and Debeney had agreed that the Moroccan Division would retake the old front line between Monument Farm and U.17.a.1.5, one and a half miles away on the Hangard road at the northern end of Hangard Wood West, that night if possible. 50 Battalion was to swing its line up towards the farm on the left of the Moroccans, while 10/Essex and 7/Queen's from the 18th Division seized the wood on their right. On the Luce flank, two battalions of the French 131st Division would attack Hangard.

During the afternoon, the Moroccan reconnaissance parties could not ascertain the precise location of 54 Brigade's line. His request for a postponement to the 27th turned down and dismissing a night advance over unknown terrain as 'unthinkable', General Daugan

Moroccan troops in 1918.

rejected Butler's advice against assaulting in daylight across the open plain east of Cachy and opted to attack from the Domart road, just ahead of which 54 Brigade's line was thought to run, at 5.15 am on 26 April. He called for a creeping barrage starting well to the east of the road, where the Germans were given to be.

'Great panache, the sounding of trumpets and beating of drums, terrible losses and hardly any territorial gain', such was the Moroccan Division's attack. The Tirailleurs and the Foreign Legion in the centre and on the right were shocked to see the Germans in the misty light to the west of the Domart road while the barrage fell uselessly on the other side. Suffering dreadfully, they managed to cross over but a counterattack by 78 and 91 IR hurled them back. It was stopped only by the timely arrival of three British tanks.

On the left, fire from Monument Farm and Wood prevented any advance by 50 Battalion. The Zouaves stopped next to them after passing through the 51st and the 52nd, although one group somehow pushed forward a few hundred yards to the Hangard road quarry and secured *Elfriede*. A second attack by the Zouaves, planned for 8.45 am, was called off when the German fire could not be suppressed. All told, the Moroccan Division lost nearly 3,500 men. The 131st Division failed at Hangard.

Hampered by German shelling and unsure where the front line was, 10/Essex on the left and 7/Queen's on the right formed up in some confusion behind the Cachy-Hangard road for their attack on Hangard Wood West. The barrage was ragged and missed much of the wood, especially in front of the Essex, who had to take most of it. Appearing soon after, the three tanks 'besides drawing machine gun fire and bombs, made no material difference to the advance'. Both battalions struggled through the dense undergrowth, which rendered the German machine gunners and snipers almost invisible. Lieutenant Colonel T.M Banks, 10/Essex's commanding officer, was with its third wave:

Ping! went something through my boot and a sting in the big toe announced a gold stripe. Hit number one! . . . Bullets fairly zipping round, and vicious cracklings from all sides from Boche concealed in the brushwood. Found that we were properly held up in one corner; and the French suddenly started a rearward movement, which was spreading panic-like to our men; but managed to stem this and we held the ground gained. Nothing for it but to get the men busy, when bang! Another bullet through the fringe of my sleeve, grazing my wrist . . . another rapid tear in my sleeve announced a third hit.

Some of the Essex reached the Hangard road on the far side of the wood but were never heard from again. 'Considerably decimated', the rest dug in behind the raised bank of the main north-south drive, where the Queen's joined them. Together they had retaken half of Hangard Wood West, the day's only worthwhile gain.[8]

The Last Act

Butler was most concerned that Monument Farm and Wood remained in German hands because they provided a springboard for another assault on Villers-Bretonneux and enfiladed any advance towards Hangard Wood. Late in the afternoon, he ordered Heneker to complete without delay the original task of retaking the old front line either side of the railway to remove the threat. Given the fate of the French attack, Glasgow told Lieutenant Colonel Armitage that another daylight advance was crazy but Armitage said Butler had insisted. Elliott complained to Hobbs that it was 'a harebrained suggestion'. The two Australian brigades were then instructed to send out reconnaissance patrols. If they reported a daylight advance was impossible, it would be undertaken that night. When 1/Worcs and 1/Sherwood Foresters, which had also been slated for the attack, said their men were not fit, it was cancelled.

Elliott could now eliminate the German salient in 15 Brigade's line on Hill 104. At 2.19 am on 27 April, a Stokes mortar lobbed twelve bombs onto the nearest German machine gun, located at P.19.central, and twelve more on another one behind it. B and D Companies from 60 Battalion attacked a minute later but the Germans reacted just as swiftly, their flares illuminating the scene for the machine gunners further back. The fire was the hottest some veterans had experienced. B Company on the right promptly charged the Germans, who fled across the Hamel road, but D Company on the left had to rush their posts one at a time. At 2.40 pm, 60 Battalion's line

Lieutenant John Simpson. John McKenna

136

joined the flank of the 54th. At 8 am, the 60th and the artillery scattered the Germans as they assembled south of Vaire Wood for a counterattack.

This attack and the steady German shelling of the Hamel road afterwards cost 60 Battalion almost 100 men, more than the counterattack two nights before. Among the dead was D Company's commander, Lieutenant Simpson. Invalided to Australia after his right arm was almost severed at Fromelles in July 1916, he returned a year later, his arm virtually paralysed and his hand covered by a woollen mitten because it always felt cold. Boxing one handed and captaining one of its football teams, Simpson had become an institution in 15 Brigade and his loss was deeply felt.

The final phase of the month long drama at Villers-Bretonneux was now over. No German set foot in it again except as a prisoner of war, the 5th Division's history proudly noted. On 26/27 April, the French took over III Corps' line as far as the positions opposite Monument Farm and, on the following night, 4 and 12 Brigades from the 4th Australian Division began relieving 13 and 15 Brigades and the 8th Division around the town. To make sure it was held and to ensure a

An Australian digger and a French poilu enjoy each other's company.

firm junction with the French at what became International Post, Haig directed that the Australian Corps and III Corps swap places. The Australian Corps was to remain between Villers-Bretonneux and the Ancre on the Fourth Army's – and the BEF's – left flank, and III Corps on its return from relief would take over the old Australian line north of the Ancre.[9]

NOTES

1. *OH*, pp. 579-80, 590-1, 595; N. Browning, *Fix Bayonets* (Browning, 2000), pp. 159, 164.
2. Entry and Report dated 25 April 1918, 15 Bde WD; McMullin, op. cit., p. 409; A.D. Ellis, *The Story of the Fifth Australian Division* (Hodder and Stoughton, 1920); entries for 24 April 1918: 59 Bn WD, Item 23/76, Roll 98; 60 Bn WD, Item 23/77, Roll 99; AWM 4.
3. *OH*, p. 603; Downing, op. cit., p. 118-9; A.S.K. Rusden, undated account, 12/11/888, 1DRL 559, AWM; 57 Bn WD, 24-5 April 1918, Item 23/74, Roll 94, AWM.
4. 9/Londons and 7/Beds WD, 24-5 April 1918, WO 95/3009 and 95/2043, TNA; 'Operations 24-7 April 1918', 7/RW Kents WD; P.H. Liddle, *The Soldiers' War*, 1914-1918 (Blandford, 1988), p. 224.
5. Mason, *Memoir*, pp. 95-6; 2/Northants and 22/DLI WD, 24-5 April 1918, WO 95/1702 and 95/1722, TNA; Elliott to 5 Div, 29 April 1918, 15 Bde WD.
6. Mason, *Memoir*, pp. 98-103; *OH*, pp. 626-7;
7. 2/Northants WD, 25 April, WO 95/1722, TNA.
8. Blaxland, op. cit., p. 130, Nichols, op. cit., pp. 330-1; 'Report on Ops 24-27 April 1918, 10/Essex WD, WO 95/2038, TNA; 7/Queen's Report, undated, WD, April 1918, WO 95/2051, TNA.
9. Elliott to J.Treloar, 7 July 1918, 15 Bde WD; Report dated 28 April 1918, 60 Bn WD; Ellis, op. cit., p. 301.

Chapter Eight

AFTERMATH

The battle cost 15 Brigade 455 men and 13 Brigade 1,009. When 14 Brigade's casualties and those gassed during the German bombardment were added, the Australian losses came to 2,473 men. In III Corps, the 8th Division had 3,553 casualties, the 18th Division 2,446 and the 58th Division 3,530, making a total of 9,529 men, of whom 2,400 were taken prisoner. The German losses amounted to almost 3,000 for the 77th Reserve Division, 2,000 for the 4th Guards, around 1,500 in the 228th and under 500 for the 243rd. Another 614 men were prisoners. Lieutenant George Mitchell of 48 Battalion saw what these figures meant when 12 Brigade took over the line south of the Roman Road:

> *Villers standing in gloomy grandeur on our left, smoke rising from shells and many fires... All about us lay the dead, pitifully boyish-looking Tommies who had been driven out of Villers. Among them were the equipments of our 13th and 15th Brigade men who had died in the recapture of Villers and had been buried... The price to the enemy was shown in the grey-clad clusters of dead.*
>
> *A Digger came to me with a sandbag, half-filled. 'I found this by a dead bloke. Have a look over it'... Very few things contained so much tragedy as the contents of that sandbag. They were all*

German dead after the battle.

letters, unsealed and uncensored. Some of the letters were pierced through and crimson-stained... I could see everything clearly. These were the letters written by our 13th and 15th Brigade men before they were rushed into the attack. Without a chance to post them, they had carried them on to battle. And they had died. The unknown gatherer had been struck down during his kindly task.

Now the sacred duty had fallen to me, from the hand of death, to deal rightly by them. Long I pondered the problem. It would not be fair to just frank and send them on. False hopes might be raised that the sender still lived... That afternoon I spent writing a short explanatory note on each letter. I strove for words to ease the blow, yet did not attempt to raise vain hopes.

The trade-off was the saving of Villers-Bretonneux a second time and hence the removal of the threat to Amiens. As it was almost entirely due to the Australian counterattack, the Australian casualties, Bean wrote later, 'if fairly severe, brought a result out of all proportion to their severity'.[1]

Bouquets and Brickbats

Coming as it did after the Germans had been making the running for over a month, the triumph raised the Australians' fighting reputation even higher. Foch spoke afterwards of their 'altogether astonishing valiance' in the counterattack. On the British side, Brigadier General Grogan, who fought alongside them, called it 'perhaps the greatest individual feat of the war'. His staff captain, Philip Ledward, commented: 'They just went forward, each man for himself, in the way that only they had mastered'. Another British officer, Major Neville Lytton, wrote:

The importance of Villers-Bretonneux cannot be over-estimated. The Australians... made one of the most astounding manoeuvres of the war... the battlefield discipline of the Australians must be absolutely perfect, no matter what their billet discipline might be... Even if the Australians achieved nothing else in this war but [its] recapture, they would have won the right to be considered among the greatest fighting races of the world.[2]

Among the Australians, the derisive estimate of British troops had hardened since the first battle. In mid-April, Monash sent his wife popular jokes that were 'strongly illustrative' of the Australian attitude:

A Brigadier of a British Brigade when 'withdrawing' before

German weapons captured by 15 Brigade.

> *the recent Bosch advance, caught up with a rabbit, which was racing along in front of him. 'Get out of the way, you brute', said he, 'and make way for somebody who can run'.*

Writing home on 26 April, Monash's tone was one of tiresome resignation:

> *It was the same old story. My 9th Brigade had held securely, and kept the Bosch out of the town of Villers-Bretonneux for three weeks. They were then withdrawn for a rest on April 23rd, and the 8th British Division (regulars) took over the sector from them.*
>
> *Naturally, on April 24th, the Bosch attacked... and biffed the Tommies out of the town. Late at night we had to organise a counter-attack. This was undertaken by 13th and 15th Brigades, in the early hours of Anzac Day. They advanced 3,000 yards, in the dark, without Artillery support, completely restored the position, and captured over 1,000 prisoners... It was a fine performance.*

Himself British-born and, unlike Monash, involved at first hand, Hobbs remarked: 'The conduct of some of the [British] troops through the ignorance, neglect, or I am almost tempted to say – but I won't, I'll say nervousness – of their officers has had a very depressing effect on me and disgusted many of my officers and men'. Elliott was incensed by the congratulatory message III Corps issued after the attack, which stated: 'The brilliant idea of the 3rd Corps for the recapture of Villers-

Bretonneux was ably carried out by the 8th Division, assisted by the 13th and 15th Australian Infantry Brigades'. The 5th Division laughed at this 'complacent and extraordinary remark'. At the end of April, matters had reached a point where Birdwood felt impelled to urge senior Australian commanders to do their utmost to put a stop to 'disparaging comparisons' between Dominion and British troops:

> *The Dominion soldier has so established his merits that depreciation of his kith and kin is not necessary for the full acknowledgement of the great work Dominion troops are doing. We are of the same blood, and the creation of friction by criticism is only playing the German's game.[3]*

A Soldier's Fight

As on 4 April, the performance of the British divisions at Second Villers-Bretonneux was patchy. The reasons were the same and made the Australian criticism only partly justified. Still recovering from the heavy fighting at the start of the *Michael* offensive, they consisted of 'children' with a leavening of tired veterans, all commanded by largely untried junior officers.

The 18th Division was more involved at Villers-Bretonneux than any other. It fought in both battles and contributed to the defensive operations between them, while its battalions participated in at least eight attacks or counterattacks from 2-26 April. True, 54 Brigade's counterattack on the 24th failed, but it had no landmarks such as the fires in the town to guide it and the battalions were never in touch. Even so, 7/Bedfords under 2/Lieutenant Tysoe helped 13 Brigade by keeping its right flank reasonably secure. By taking and holding half of Hangard Wood West, 7/Queen's and 10/Essex scored the only decent success in the counterstroke on 26 April. Two days earlier, 2/10 Londons from the 58th Division had launched a counterattack towards the wood that strengthened 173 Brigade's resolve to keep Cachy after parts of it had fallen back before the tanks supporting the 77th Reserve Division. The efforts overall of the 18th and 58th Divisions on III Corps' right flank were significant, especially as the French were not always as helpful as they might have been.

Defending the town, the 8th Division faced the 4th Guards and the 228th Divisions, decidedly superior formations to the 77th Reserve. It also bore the brunt of the German tank attack and 23 Brigade, the hardest hit formation, had not seen in daylight the ground it was defending. For all this, the 8th, the principal target of Monash's ire, 'did not have its finest hour at Second Villers-Bretonneux'. Like the

14th (Light) in the first battle, it gave way very quickly, creating the crisis. Elliott found 22/DLI singularly unimpressive but praised 2/R. Berks, who did much of the Durhams' job in the mopping-up phase. 'Well done Royal Berks', a congratulatory message from the 5th Division said. 2/Northants also showed great spirit and initiative while attached to 13 Brigade.

Compared to the British divisions, the Australians were in magnificent fettle. They had missed all but *Michael's* last gasps and they did not have to face tanks. Their battalions oozed experience, which yielded the tactical prowess that enabled them to attack at night over unknown ground, something not even the elite Moroccan Division was willing to do. They practised bayonet fighting assiduously, achieving a superiority that made many Germans reluctant to face them once they got close. Bean describes the admiration of an officer in the 228th Division for the tactical *nous* shown by the part of 15 Brigade's line that his section of four machine guns engaged:

> The line dropped, but, as soon as the guns were turned elsewhere, it rose and advanced again. He swung his guns around to meet it, and again it dropped. This happened three or four times, and then he found an Australian machine-gun firing from behind his flank. Thus, he said, the attack was on his troops

Australians on Hill 104 with Villers-Bretonneux being shelled in the background. One wounded man is heading rearwards. The umbrella has been put to good use.

*and round them and past them before they realised that they were
confronted by a critical situation.*

As Elliott readily acknowledged, it was at this level that the battle was
won:

> *The fight became a soldiers' fight purely and simply, and
> neither myself nor the Battalion Commanders could exercise any
> control upon it. The success was due to the energy and
> determination of junior commanders and the courage of the
> troops.[4]*

Command Decisions

In his praise of the Australians, Foch remarked that the high command
had 'merely the task of living up to the standard imposed by such
soldiers'. At Hangard Wood, those soldiers could not overcome their
commanders' poor appreciation of ground and rushed planning. At
Villers-Bretonneux, the commanders' task was to counterattack as
soon as possible because the longer they took, the stronger the German
defences became. Lieutenant Colonel Goddard grasped the necessity
in the first battle by ordering 36 Battalion to counterattack
immediately he knew that the German afternoon attack had broken
through. The task was not so well handled in the second.

All the intelligence in the few days before 24 April indicated that a
very strong attack was coming. Given the convalescent state of the 8th
Division, another German breakthrough was at least a possibility, in
which case the designated counterattack battalions, 2/R. Berks and
2/Devons, would swing into action. Not only was their condition no
different to the rest of the division but the Devons were also recovering
from the effects of gas. Elliott and Hobbs had realised from the start
that the 8th Division would need help and Elliott's brigade, ideally
located and, thanks to his foresight, drilled to counterattack the town,
was best placed to provide it. But Heneker and Butler thought outside
assistance unnecessary, so no contingency plan existed if the need for
it actually arose.

Heneker initially treated the news that the Germans had taken the
town as alarmist. Through his patrols and liaison officers, Elliott knew
the truth well before Heneker and stood by to counterattack from the
early hours. When Hobbs gave him qualified approval to do so at 8.40
am, the mist still lingered and the Germans, not having had time to
organise their defence, were vulnerable. By then, the 8th Division was
no longer a cohesive formation. Nonetheless, Butler and Heneker
turned down Hobbs's offer of 15 Brigade, stating that the 8th could

handle things. British tanks helped stabilise the situation but the 8th Division's attempts to eject the Germans from Villers-Bretonneux came down to a failed counterattack by 1/Sherwood Foresters around midday.

Fortunately, Rawlinson insisted on Australian involvement in the town's recapture, resulting in a backflip by Butler and Heneker, who gave 13 Brigade the very job they had hitherto argued the 8th Division was quite capable of doing alone. Heneker recommended a night counterattack but acquiesced when Butler, under pressure from Rawlinson to go earlier, settled on 8 pm, though it was still light then. Glasgow argued heatedly with Heneker to win a postponement until 10 pm. After his reconnaissance, he also refused to attack on the axis Butler specified, stunning Heneker again. Remaining at Glisy, Heneker was out of touch. His post-battle narrative even stated that 23 Brigade had cleared the Bois d'Aquenne so that the counterattack was not interfered with from it at all. In fact, the Germans there carved up 13 Brigade until Lieutenant Sadlier's attack removed them. 23 Brigade, with the help of tanks, did not clear the wood until next day.

Hobbs, meanwhile, received no details of 15 Brigade's likely role until the mid-afternoon, even though Rawlinson had told Butler at 11.30 am to brief him regarding a counterattack either side of the town. Historians have excused the delay on the grounds that 13 Brigade's part had not yet been finalised. A soldier would make no such allowance because the delay precluded concurrent battle procedure within 15 Brigade. Armed with even the broadest outline of the plan, Elliott could have issued relevant preliminary orders much earlier, completed administrative arrangements and so on, and the battalions, companies and platoons of 15 Brigade done the same. It would have saved time later.

Elliott probably did not see Heneker during the afternoon, though Bean said he did in the Australian Official History. Bean wrote it after Elliott's death and then realised that the statements of the surviving participants disagreed. He was never able to clarify the issue. Elliott did not mention a meeting in his diary or in his writings on the battle and there is no record of one in the communication logs. 15 Brigade did not pass to Heneker's command until 9.5 pm, which also makes a meeting unlikely. Hence Elliott had little idea of 13 Brigade's arrangements until he saw Glasgow at 8 pm, and their hurried co-ordination resulted in a significant last minute change to what was supposed to be the final plan. By consistently leaving it outside the loop, Butler and Heneker ensured that 15 Brigade, which had been ready to counterattack since early morning, did so almost two hours late. The irony was absurd.

Glasgow emerges as the outstanding commander of the battle, although Elliott mildly criticised him for allowing 13 Brigade to pass too close to the Bois d'Aquenne, where 'its driving power was lost'. As Elliott admitted, however, Glasgow had been told the wood was clear. Elliott himself did not ensure his commanders understood that the final objective was further east than the one given in his provisional orders. On the other hand, his disposition of 15 Brigade's right flank set it up to clear the town promptly. According to Bean, he would have attacked in daylight on the 24th, which made Heneker's decision to do so at night extremely fortuitous. Conversely, both Butler and Heneker wanted the Australians to assault in daylight on 26 April, an undertaking that Elliott and Glasgow strenuously – and successfully – opposed.[5]

Butler, who had to deal only with Hobbs, graciously acknowledged the contribution of 13 and 15 Brigades. From Heneker, a strong-willed man who ran up against equally strong-willed men in Hobbs, Glasgow and Elliott, not a word of appreciation was forthcoming. Personalities aside, the way many of the decisions were reached, largely through the interaction between the divisional and brigade commanders, illustrated the trend towards a devolved system of tactical command in the BEF that the German offensive had accelerated. Villers-Bretonneux took the process a stage further and, in the second half of 1918, it was one of the keys to victory during the great advance of the Hundred Days.

Never Forget Australia
Like Cachy, Villers-Bretonneux at the end of the battle was 'a mere heap of road mending material'. The red chateau, though 'perfectly knocked about', was the most intact building. A faint smell of onions lingered, the legacy of mustard gas, and the cats it had killed still littered the town three months later. The Australians were bloodily repulsed at Monument Farm and Wood in early May but took them in July using 'peaceful penetration'. On 4 July, Hamel fell to the first true all-arms attack. It had been meticulously planned by General Monash and was his first operation as commander of the Australian Corps. Elsewhere, the line either side of the Roman Road remained largely static until the famous attack on 8 August, in which the Australians and Canadians had the main role and III Corps assaulted on the far bank of the Somme.

After the war, close ties sprang up between Villers-Bretonneux and

Villers-Bretonneux church then...

... and now.

the Australian state of Victoria, from whence the battalions of 15 Brigade came. Melbourne adopted the town and Victorians contributed to its reconstruction. Donations from Victorian schoolchildren funded the rebuilding of the primary school, which reopened in 1923. Part of it is called *Salle Victoria*. Since the 1970s the school has housed the ANZAC Museum, which is dedicated to the AIF and its operations, particularly those on the Somme in 1918. An Australian Room inside the *mairie*, built on the site of the destroyed white château in the town centre, displays the town's Australian links. In 1984 Villers-Bretonneux was twinned with the Victorian town of Robinvale.

Australian and British soldiers rest alongside each other in the grounds of the Australian National Memorial on Hill 104 and in the surrounding cemeteries, a silent reminder that, although the Australian role was decisive, the British were also heavily involved in the month long saga that Captain – later Major General – Essame called 'one of the most sanguinary actions of the war'. The red château, which housed an aid post until the Australian Graves Unit took it over, stood

The plaque on the wall of the Villers-Bretonneux primary school.

derelict as a mute witness to the battle and, indeed, the war on the Western Front, until August 2004, when it was demolished to make way for a supermarket. The mayor of Villers-Bretonneux, whom the Australian government honoured with an award in 2000, reportedly said after the demolition that the château was of no historical value. *Mephisto* is on display in the Queensland Museum at Southbank, Brisbane, the sole surviving A7V *Kampfwagen*. The Australians found the tank where it had come to grief in Monument Wood.[6]

For Australians themselves, there is one other reminder of what their countrymen did at Villers-Bretonneux in 1918 and in the years that followed. At the school and in the *mairie* appear the words *N'oublions jamais l'Australie* – 'Never Forget Australia' – for all to see. Pity that memory did not extend to the red château, which can be seen no more.

NOTES

1. G.D. Mitchell, *Backs To The Wall* (Angus & Robertson, 1937), pp. 210-11; *OH*, p. 637.

2. *OH*, pp. 638; N. Lytton, *The Press and the General Staff* (Collins, 1920), pp. 163-4; M. Brown, *The Imperial War Museum Book of 1918* (Sidgwick & Jackson, 1998), p. 105.

3. Monash to wife 16 April 1918, Monash Papers, MS 1184, National Library of Australia, and 26 April, DRL 2316, AWM; Hobbs, D, 27 April 1918, PR 82/153/3, AWM; Elliott to J.Treloar, 7 July 1918, 15 Bde WD; P. Simkins, 'The Absolute Limit', unpublished paper, p. 2.

4. 'Absolute Limit', p. 26; *OH*, 641-2; McMullin, op. cit., pp. 409-10.

5. 8 Div Narrative; Elliott to Monash, 18 September 1929, DRL 3856, AWM; *OH*, p. 639.

6. Nicholls, op. cit., p. 312; R.M. Keegan, 'An Even Break', pp. 8-7/8, MSS 1333, AWM; J. Bull, Beloved of the Valkyries, p. 251, MS 1359, AWM; Essame, op. cit., p. 49.

Mephisto after its capture by the Australians in Monument Wood.

Mephisto in the Queensland Museum at Southbank, Brisbane.

Chapter Nine

CEMETERIES AND MEMORIALS

The cemeteries around Villers-Bretonneux range from isolated graves through extensions of communal graveyards to large postwar concentration cemeteries. Captain Bushelle of 36 Battalion, killed on 6 April 1918, for example, lies in Grave 40 of the 43 burials in **Blangy-Tronville Communal Cemetery Extension**, which is across the railway south of the village. His commanding officer, Lieutenant Colonel Milne, rests at VIII.J.19 in **Heath Cemetery** at Harbonnières, a few kilometres east of the battlefield. Others, such as Lieutenant Colonel McConaghy of 54 Battalion at I.J.31 in **Namps-au-Val British Cemetery** and Lieutenant Colonel Symonds of 2/10 Londons at D.19 in **Picquigny British Cemetery**, lie near Amiens. Brigadier Forster, who led 42 Brigade, and Lieutenant Colonel Dewing of 8/R. Berks, are commemorated on the **Pozières Memorial to the Missing**, a couple of kilometres north of Albert.

1,610 French soldiers rest in **Marcelcave Buttes National Cemetery**, 1.3 kilometres northwest of Marcelcave. Most of them died in 1916 in Evacuation Hospital No. 13, which was set up alongside the railway nearby. Major Carr commanded A Company, 33 Battalion from the cemetery on 4 April 1918.

Perhaps the most poignant burial in the area is that of Lieutenant Thompson of 18 Battalion, who lies alone in **Cachy Communal Cemetery**. The sadness evoked by his lonely grave raises the question of why he was not laid to rest among his fellow Australians in nearby Adelaide or Crucifix Corner Cemeteries.

The grave of Lieutenant Harold Thompson.

Adelaide Cemetery

Situated on the N29 on the western outskirts of Villers-Bretonneux, Adelaide Cemetery was begun in June 1918 near an advanced dressing station. Plot I is the site of the original cemetery and 864 graves from smaller cemeteries were concent-

Adelaide Cemetery in the late 1920s with memorial crosses in the left foreground.

The grave of
Lieutenant Colonel
Stephen Latham.

rated around it after the Armistice. Of the 954 burials, 519 are Australian, 365 British, 22 Canadian and 48 unknown. The Villers-Bretonneux dead include Lieutenant Colonel Latham of 2/Northants at II.G.13. 13 Brigade, its four battalions and 22/DLI all erected wooden crosses in the cemetery to commemorate their fallen from the battle. 51 Battalion's cross was taken back to Australia in 1933 and is now in St George's Cathedral, Perth. On 11 November 1993, the remains of an Australian unknown exhumed from III.M.13 were reinterred as the 'Unknown Australian Soldier' in the Hall of Memory at the Australian War Memorial in Canberra.

Crucifix Corner Cemetery

Located on the D23 on the southern side of the A29 autoroute, the site of this cemetery figured prominently in both battles. The first burials were Canadian dead from the great attack on 8 August 1918. Closing at the end of August, the cemetery reopened postwar as a concentration cemetery. Of the 660 Commonwealth graves, 236 are Australian with another Sixty Australian unknowns, and Seventy-six are Canadian. Almost the entire left side is given over to 141 French graves, which face east like the British graves alongside them, symbolising the joint effort of the two armies to stem the German tide in the spring of 1918 before the advance to victory began from the area in the summer. A tablet placed by the locals commemorates 'the heroes who died in the defence of Villers-Bretonneux'. One of them, Lieutenant Simpson of 60 Battalion, rests at V.B.6.

The Villers-Bretonneux memorial tablet in Crucifix Corner Cemetery.

The grave of Lieutenant John Simpson.

Hangard Communal Cemetery Extension

The communal cemetery was the scene of incessant fighting from 4 April onwards and changed hands frequently. The Canadians finally captured it on 8 August and started the extension, recovering Thirty-two dead who had lain in the open since April. They rest on the left near the road in Plot I. Postwar concentrations, which consisted mainly of dead from the Hangard and Hangard Wood battles, increased the number of burials to 553, of whom over half are unknowns. The cemetery is located on the D76 on the eastern edge of Hangard.

Hangard Wood British Cemetery

This cemetery's location near the southeastern corner of Hangard Wood West was on the British front line until the Germans took most of the wood on 24 April. The Canadians regained it on 8 August and began the cemetery later that month. Their original burials are in Plot I and include Private John Croak VC at I.A.9. They also recovered dead from the April fighting, identifying some as men from the 18th Division. Laid to rest in Plot II, they were joined after the war by seven Australian dead from Villers-Bretonneux and dead from elsewhere on the Somme. The cemetery now contains 141 Commonwealth burials from the First World War, Thirty-nine of which are unidentified, and Fourteen French burials. It is best reached by taking the sealed road north from Hangard and turning right after 1.6 kilometres onto the

Hangard Wood British Cemetery.

track that skirts the southern edge of the wood.

Toronto Cemetery

Marooned in the fields at the end of a rough track off the D42 two kilometres north of Démuin, this cemetery must be one of the loneliest on the Western Front. Begun by the Canadians after 8 August and mostly comprising their dead, it is of interest because it stands on the line held by 1/78 IR and facing Lancer Wood that 33 Battalion and 12/Lancers attacked on 30 March.

Villers-Bretonneux Military Cemetery and Australian National Memorial

The lasting fame the Australians won at Villers-Bretonneux made it their inevitable choice as the location for a national memorial. Its construction was anything but inevitable. In 1927, Melbourne architect William Lucas won the design competition for a memorial that was to be built from Australian materials and cost no more than £100,000. The depression struck before work started and the Scullin Labour government abandoned the project on the grounds that it was unaffordable. In 1935, embarrassment that Australia was still without a memorial led to its resurrection but at the reduced cost of £30,000, which meant an entirely new design using local materials. The last of

Toronto Cemetery.

The dedication of the Australian National Memorial on 22 July 1938.

the Dominion memorials to be unveiled, it was dedicated by King George VI on 22 July 1938.

Rising from the western end of Hill 104 on the D23, Sir Edward Lutyens' creation features a tower 100 feet high that offers terrific views and has an orientation table with directions and distances to places as far away as Gallipoli and Canberra. The screen walls flanking the tower enshrine the names of the 10,982 Australians killed in France (except for the 1,298 listed at VC Corner Cemetery at Fromelles) who have no known grave. Lieutenant Frewin of 18 Battalion, who fell at Cemetery Copse on 15 April, and Captain Morgan of the 57th, killed on 25 April, are among them. Overlooked by the Memorial, the cemetery was established postwar as a concentration cemetery. With the graves of 1,089 British soldiers, 779 Australians, 267 Canadians, Four South Africans and Two New Zealanders, it is the largest on the 1918 Somme battlefields. Major Craies of 52 Battalion, who also fell on 25 April, lies at X.E.9.

The Memorial and Cemetery were damaged in June 1940 when a

Viller-Bretonneux Military Cemetery and Australian National Memorial.

German tank crashed through the lower right hand corner of the cemetery and engaged a French machine gun crew in the tower, which a Bf 109 also strafed for good measure. Spalling on the Cross of Sacrifice and some of the headstones remain as honourable scars of war. If it is not open, the keys to the tower can be obtained from the gendarmerie. A ceremony is held annually at the Memorial on Anzac Day, 25 April.

The Australian Corps Memorial Park
Set amongst some of the original German trenches on the Wolfsberg, this memorial owes much to the late John Laffin, a prolific Australian military historian who fought in New Guinea during the Second World War. He waged a forty-year crusade for an Australian memorial park similar to those of the Canadians on Vimy Ridge, the Newfoundlanders at Beaumont-Hamel and the South Africans at Delville Wood, and to the British Memorial to the Missing at Thiepval. He lived long enough to see his vision realised when the Memorial was opened on 4 July 1998, the 70th anniversary of the capture of Hamel and the Wolfsberg by the Australian Corps under General Monash.

Commemorating the achievements of the Australian Corps, the Memorial consists of three curved walls of black granite, into which Melbourne stonemason Colin Anderson sandblasted the Australian Rising Sun badge, a likeness of Monash and scenes from the attack on 8 August 1918, in which the Corps featured prominently. Colour patches from every Australian unit have been glazed onto the top of the low encompassing walls and glass information panels in the trenches explain significant points in English and French. Ceremonies are held at the Memorial on July 4 or, if that day falls during the week, on the first weekend after.

The Australian Corps Memorial Park.

Chapter Ten

BATTLEFIELD TOURS

The Villers-Bretonneux battlefield is hardly compact. Hangard is ten kilometres south of Vaire-sous-Corbie and Lamotte-Warfusée is eight kilometres east of the Bois l'Abbé. Shortcuts and access are not what they were because of the changes to the road and track network necessitated by the new A29 autoroute. While these considerations by no means preclude a rewarding drive or walk, they do make vantage points more important.

The Wolfsberg

The Australian Corps Memorial Park on the Wolfsberg is an excellent location from which to study the fighting on the Somme flank. The Amiens Inner Defence Line straddled it and headed south past the left of Accroche/Arquaire Wood to cross the Roman Road near Lamotte-Warfusée, the village on the skyline next to the wood. Occupied by Carey's Force on 26 March, the Inner Line was the last line of defence before Villers-Bretonneux. Next day, the Australians manning it above Sailly-le-Sec, due north on the far bank of the Somme, watched the cavalry screen prevent 1 Grenadier Regiment and 43 IR gaining the near bank. Resistance was especially stubborn in Sailly-Laurette, the village next to Sailly-le-Sec.

Unable to progress, 43 IR crossed at Cerisy, four kilometres east of the Wolfsberg and easily seen with binoculars. Lamotte-Warfusée fell soon after. Attacking your location on 28 March, 43 IR and I/3 Grenadiers were smashed as they emerged from the Vallée d'Abancourt, the deep re-entrant in front. Part of the southern shoulder of the Wolfsberg was briefly lost on the 29th. In the general attack on 30 March, the 4th Guard and 228th Divisions assaulted between the Somme and the N29 – the Roman Road. They were easily repulsed by 1 Cavalry Brigade and Carey's men but the line above Hamel

Looking east from the Wolfsberg towards Cerisy, where 43 IR and III/3 Grenadier crossed the Somme.

Cerisy

Vallée d'Abancourt

crumpled. The Germans streamed over the Wolfsberg and into the village but a counterattack led by 5/Dragoon Guards ejected them.

The 14th (Light) Division took over the Inner Line north of the N29 on 3/4 April. 42 Brigade deployed 9/Rifle Brigade on the left and 5/Ox and Bucks on the right of the 2.4 kilometre stretch from Bouzencourt, a few buildings on the Somme flats at the end of the northerly road from Hamel, to Arquaire Wood. 7 and then 8/Rifle Brigades of 41 Brigade covered the 2.4 kilometres from there to the N29. 43 Brigade in reserve was on Hill 104, the high ground to the west, where the tower of the Australian National Memorial is visible on the skyline.

The bombardment next morning fell heaviest on 41 Brigade, which broke shortly after the 228th Division assaulted at 7 am. It regrouped near the road that runs south from Hamel between Accroche/Arquaire Wood and Hamel/Vaire Wood to the southwest. Despite reinforcement, it could not hold there either and the survivors were in 43 Brigade's line on Hill 104 by 10 am. Probing towards the Wolfsberg, 10/Hussars met the full force of 5 Guard Grenadiers, who had followed the 228th Division's attack and were swinging northwest through Hamel/Vaire Wood. The Hussars tried to grab the eastern end of Hamel Wood but were beaten back.

Worried about being cut off, 42 Brigade across the Wolfsberg disintegrated. Brigadier General Forster fell in Hamel after trying to stop his men back-pedalling over the Somme flats past Bouzencourt to Vaire, the village to the northwest on the near bank. Captain Ferres' Australians there held off the pursuing Germans and rallied enough men to dig a line of posts along the road that runs from Vaire up Hill 104. They linked with 10/Hussars on the feature near the lone tree on the skyline due west of Hamel. Artillery firing over open sights from the crest and in enfilade from across the river stopped a breakthrough during the afternoon.

The twin towers of St-Pierre Church dominate Corbie, the headquarters of 15 Brigade, which took over the 3.6 kilometre frontage from Vaire to opposite Vaire Wood. 6 Cavalry Brigade went from there to the N29. On 5 April, three German attacks over the spur that curves from Vaire Wood to the Wolfsberg were crushed and Corporal Sayers' party from 58 Battalion ambushed a German patrol midway between Bouzencourt and Vaire. Using 'peaceful penetration' thereafter, the Australians advanced their line across the flats to the western edge of Bouzencourt. The German line began near the hamlet but cut straight to Hamel, which it skirted before tracking west to join the sunken road across the facing slope of Hill 104 and then swinging around the far side of Vaire Wood.

Monument Farm/Crucifix Corner

This area is centred on the roundabout where the road from the industrial zone joins the D23 near the bridge over the A29 autoroute. Crucifix Corner Cemetery is on the right of the old stretch of the D23 at the southern end of the bridge. Marcelcave, 3.5 kilometres east, can be seen to the right of the gravel works dead ahead, while Cachy lies 3 kilometres in the opposite direction. The Bois d'Aquenne spills past the far end of Villers-Bretonneux towards it. To the south, Lancer Wood is on the left of the D23 and Hangard Wood the right.

The scrubby line to the north is the railway, and the Ferme de la Couture, enclosed by trees, is on the left of the D23 midway between it and the roundabout. It was known as Monument Farm because of the monument, a chapel built opposite on land donated by the farm owner to commemorate the defence of Villers-Bretonneux during the Franco-Prussian War in 1870. Paid for by the families of the dead, it was unveiled in 1872, destroyed in 1918, rebuilt in the 1930s with war reparation monies and razed by the farm owner in the 1970s when it had fallen into ruin. Monument Wood, the orchard around the monument, began 300 metres from the roundabout, extended 360 metres along the road and 500 metres into the field on the right. Set within a smaller orchard, the farmhouse accommodated the headquarters of 55 Brigade.

The Monument.

Starting on the eastern side of Lancer Wood, the 55th's line passed within a kilometre of Marcelcave, in front of which 8/E. Surreys handed over to 7/Buffs. When 11 BRIR attacked early on 4 April, the Buffs' left withdrew to the far side of the gravel works. The collapse of 8/Surreys in the afternoon attack exposed the Buffs' right. They streamed across the D23. Panicked when the bombardment drenched the farm in gas and ignited the outbuildings, 7/Queen's in reserve behind them joined the rout. Monument Farm and Wood were lost but Brigadier General Wood rallied two Queen's companies on a line that would have crossed the autoroute 650 metres west of the roundabout. They joined the counterattack launched by 36 Battalion from the hollow northwest of the farm.

Heavy fire from the farm complex made the Australians diverge either side of it. Hugging the railway, A and B Companies advanced over a kilometre and the Germans, fearing they might be cut off, abandoned the farm and wood. A machine gun at Crucifix Corner held up C Company and the Queen's, which had come around the southern side of the farm. Only C Company, further away from the gun, could get across the D23, where its right rested about 100 metres north of the roundabout. The new line curved from there past the gravel works to meet the old Australian support line 1.5 kilometres distant.

2/W. Yorks held this line when the Germans attacked on 24 April. Leading 93 RIR, *Baden I, Cyklop* and *Mephisto* ploughed through the gravel works area after trampling C Company on the railway but *Mephisto* ditched in a shellhole near the edge of Monument Wood, 350 metres northeast of the roundabout. A and B Companies, holding the line to Crucifix Corner, forced *Gretchen* to retreat and briefly halted *Herkules* before they were overrun, whereupon Tank 541 flattened the farm buildings. In depth at the hollow, D Company withdrew to the railway station. 2/E. Lancs, whose line ran from the hollow to the D23 on the far side of the farm before swinging north over the railway, were also overwhelmed.

The bank above Crucifix Corner Cemetery offers another perspective. Hangard Wood West and East are very well defined from it. When the Germans attacked on 30 March, 12/Lancers galloped from right to left across the plain to secure Lancer Wood, while 33 and 34 Battalions marched in column behind them. Forming up between the tip of Hangard Wood East and the D23, they advanced through Lancer Wood and charged the Germans in the old British line beyond it but were forced to dig in close to the eastern side of the wood.

On 4 April, 8/E. Surreys stretched from the right of 7/Buffs at a point 1.4 kilometres southeast of the cemetery to meet 7/RW Kents halfway along the front of Lancer Wood. When the 19th Division broke through during the afternoon attack, this line back-pedalled across the D23 to the forward edge of Hangard Wood West. It ran north from there to link up with 7/Queen's 300 metres west of the cemetery. The machine gun that troubled the Queen's and C Company, 36 Battalion was on the old D23 crossroads at the cemetery's southeastern corner.

On 24 April, the line north of Hangard Wood West was thrown back another kilometre when *Elfriede, Nixe, Siegfried* and *Shnuck* supported the 77th Reserve Division's assault. 2/4 Londons behind the cemetery repulsed the initial attack but gave way when the tanks arrived, causing 2/2 Londons alongside to abandon the wood. During the counterattack,

Monument Farm

The field of fire of the German machine gun at Crucifix Corner towards Monument Farm on the D23.

A Company, 51 Battalion briefly reached the D23 north of Monument Farm but III/5 Foot Guards, in reserve at the cemetery crossroads, repulsed 52 Battalion and 7/Bedfords south of it. The Foot Guards' regimental headquarters was in the field 320 metres east. A quick look at the open terrain between Hangard Wood and the autoroute shows why the Moroccan Division's attack towards the D23 on 26 April was annihilated.

The Australian National Memorial

The fighting north of Villers-Bretonneux is easily followed from the memorial tower, which rises above the western spur of Hill 104. As the tower is almost level with the summit, denoted by the trigonometric marker 1.6 kilometres eastwards, the all-round panorama explains Hill's 104's importance. Amiens and its cathedral are on the western horizon and the Thiepval Memorial to the Missing, at the centre of the 1916 Somme battlefield, breaks the northern skyline. Fouilloy, due north on the near bank of the river, drifts westwards into Aubigny, and Corbie cannot be missed on the far side.

Orchards ringed Villers-Bretonneux, across the hollow to the south, in 1918. Blending into each other along the N29 to its right are the Bois d'Aquenne, Bois l'Abbé and Bois de Blangy, all skirted by the railway on the near side of the road. Looking southeastwards past the town and then following the crest to the river, the church spires of Marcelcave and Lamotte-Warfusée, then Vaire Wood, the spire of Hamel church with the Wolfsberg behind it and, finally, Hamelet on the bank, can all be seen.

Attacking from a line that ran across the front of Marcelcave and Lamotte-Warfusée and beyond the Wolfsberg on 4 April, the Germans reached the near side of Vaire Wood. After coming up from the Bois l'Abbé, 34 Battalion shook out in the hollow and moved around the north of Villers-Bretonneux to help 6 Cavalry Brigade and 33rd

Battalion prevent them going further. The headquarters of the 14th (Light) Division, which had given way, was in Fouilloy, and the battalions of 15 Brigade moved through the village as well as through Hamelet en route to relieving the remnants on Hill 104 that evening.

Extending from the eastern corner of Villers-Bretonneux towards Hamelet, the Villers System passed 1.2 kilometres east of the Memorial, while the embryonic trenches that became the Villers Switch arced along the far lip of the hollow from the railway. Pioneer Switch followed the Memorial's southern fence as it linked the Villers System to the Aubigny Line, which tracked south from Aubigny to the Bois l'Abbé. Brigadier General Elliott kept a battalion at that end of it. The rest of 15 Brigade was dispersed on the flats around his headquarters at Blangy-Tronville, which can be picked out six kilometres due west.

Late on 24 April, the headquarters of 25 Brigade, 56, 59 and 60 Battalions and 15 Brigade's Advanced Report Centre were clustered around the Memorial site. 56th Battalion curved around behind it to face Villers-Bretonneux and the 55th overlooked the Somme on the northern slope. Part of 2/R. Berks was on the hollow opposite and what remained of the rest and of 2/Rifle Brigade were scattered between it and the old front line opposite Vaire Wood. After driving them back, the Germans had tried to take the summit of Hill 104 but the attempt was not co-ordinated with the artillery, which crumped I and III/48

IR as they emerged from the northern edge of the town.

15 Brigade counterattacked from the D523, the Fouilloy-Cachy Road, which is the next road back from the D23. 60 Battalion's left flank rested on it due west of the Memorial and 59 Battalion on the right lined the road as it ran up the hollow towards the railway.

The start of the Australian counterattack as seen from the Australian National Memorial.

Deployed behind the 59th, 57 Battalion had been in the stand-by position in the Aubigny Line. Guided by the light from the burning town, the assault passed the Memorial on its way to the first objective, the Hamelet-Villers-Bretonneux road, which bisects the slope between the Memorial and the summit. The Australians reached it uneventfully and were pivotting towards the N29 when the Germans detected them.

Flares turned night into day and all control was lost as the Australians charged into 478 IR and II/35 Fusilier. The area bounded by the Hamelet road, the summit and the town became the scene of the most ferocious bayonet assault of the war. Despite heavy machine gun fire, particularly from around the orchard on the town end of the Hamelet road, it was unstoppable. At 2 am the Australians began a rather confused reorganization along the Hamel road, 750 metres beyond the summit. Advancing at 6 am on 25 April with its right flank on the Hamelet road, 57 Battalion started clearing the town.

A Car Tour of the Battlefields and Related Areas
This tour covers the March-April fighting around Villers-Bretonneux and Hangard. After studying the April battles from the Australian National Memorial **(1)**, head north on the D23 to Fouilloy **(2)**, which was the headquarters of the 14th (Light) Division on 4 April and 14 Brigade on the 24th. Turn left onto the D1 at the T-junction and head west for 1.9 kilometres to the intersection with the D167 **(3)** on the outskirts of Aubigny. The Aubigny Line ran south from here to the Bois l'Abbé, while 15 Brigade's initial Advanced Report Centre was on the D1 300 metres east. Blangy-Tronville **(4)** is 5.6 kilometres along the D167. On 24 April, 59 and 60 Battalions left for the start line on the D523 from bivouacs between the road and the river near the village, and both Glasgow and Elliott were headquartered in the chateau.

Return to Fouilloy on the D1 and, 160 metres beyond the D23 junction, turn right onto the D71 for Hamelet **(5)**, which lies at the foot

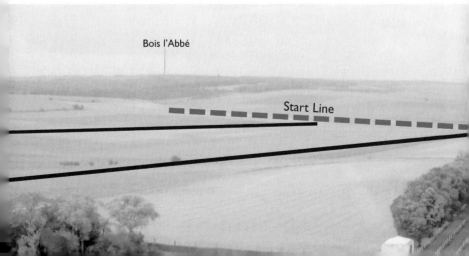

Bois l'Abbé

Start Line

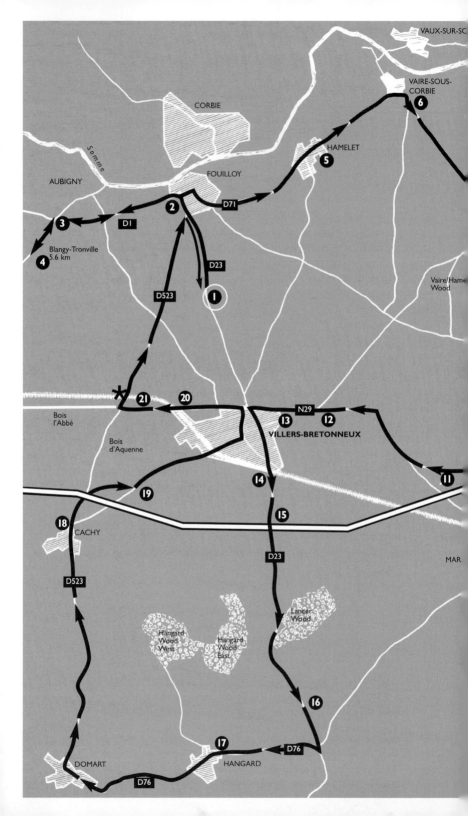

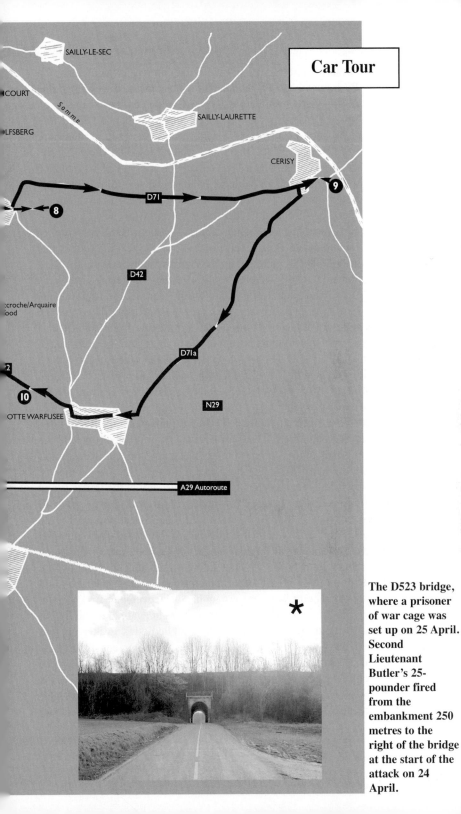

SAILLY-LE-SEC

Car Tour

COURT

Somme

SAILLY-LAURETTE

LFSBERG

CERISY

9

8

D71

D42

croche/Arquaire
ood

D71a

2

10

N29

OTTE WARFUSEE

A29 Autoroute

The D523 bridge, where a prisoner of war cage was set up on 25 April. Second Lieutenant Butler's 25-pounder fired from the embankment 250 metres to the right of the bridge at the start of the attack on 24 April.

of the northern slope of Hill 104. 15 Brigade's first objective was the Villers-Bretonneux end of the road that winds upward from the village. Now head for Vaire-sous-Corbie, the next village on the D71. Stay on this road as it turns sharp right at Vaire church and then left at the fork at a crucifix between two trees. On 4 April, 42 Brigade hurtled back towards B Company, 58th Battalion, which straddled the D71 300 metres from the outskirts (6). The Australians and 10/Hussars stopped enough of them to connect with the Hussars' left 1.4 kilometres away on the sealed road that heads up the hillside. Artillery firing from the crest helped keep 5 Guard Grenadiers from following.

By mid-April, the Australian line crossed the D71 500 metres further on and ran to Bouzencourt on the Somme two kilometres due east. Corporal Sayers' men shot up the German patrol making for Vaire on the far side of the trees to the northeast. As you head towards Hamel, Vaire and Hamel Woods are on the skyline due south. 48 IR and 35 Fusilier were battered coming over the high ground between the woods and the village on 5 April. The German line from Bouzencourt crossed the D71 as it enters Hamel (7) and ran west to the track on the far hillside. Brigadier Forster of 42 Brigade was killed in the village when it fell. Once in Hamel, follow the signs to the Australian Corps Memorial (8) on the Wolfsberg and consider the fighting on the Somme flank from it.

On leaving, turn right onto the D71 and right again 500 metres later. Sailly-le-Sec is on the far bank, Bouzencourt on the near one and the Vallée d'Abancourt, the forming-up place for the German attacks between Accroche Wood and the Somme, looms after 1.3 kilometres. Going over the D42, head into Cerisy and turn left at the traffic island and then right for the bridge (9), which was partly destroyed when 43 IR crossed on 27 March. It seized Hill 66, which overlooks the cemeteries on Cerisy's outskirts, allowing III/3 Grenadiers to drive on Lamotte. Advancing on the axis of the D71a, they trounced a weak counterattack force in the wood 1.6 kilometres distant on the left of the road. Lamotte, whose art deco church spire is unmistakeable, and Warfusée-Abancourt were in German hands by evening.

Turn right onto the N29 at the cemetery, right again onto the D42 at the traffic lights by the small church 1.1 kilometres further on, and then left onto the D122 after 150 metres. The Amiens Inner Line crossed it 500 metres westwards (10) and ran past the front of Accroche/Arquaire Woods, which you can see a kilometre north, to the Wolfsberg. Carey's Force held it until relieved by the 14th (Light) Division on 3/4 April. 7 and 8/Rifle Brigade from 41 Brigade took over

Cerisy Bridge today.

this part of the line and its third battalion, 8/KRRC, was in depth behind Accroche Wood on a rough support line on the Hamel road. Turn left onto it after a kilometre.

After collapsing early on 4 April, 7 and 8/Rifle Brigades reformed in this vicinity, buttressed by 8/KRRC and most of 9/Scottish Rifles, which had come up from Hill 104. They disintegrated again mid-morning, prompting a chaotic three-kilometre withdrawal to 43 Brigade's line there. The rot spread to 42 Brigade on the Wolfsberg. Marcelcave comes into view as you cross the N29 heading south. Attacking from it in broad daylight on 28 March, the 61st Division almost reached Lamotte-Warfusée. For the 61st's perspective, park by the autoroute flyover and look north from the bank but remember that the assault started well behind you. From here, head for Marcelcave Buttes National Cemetery **(11)**, which you can see several hundred metres west.

The demarcation stone on the N29 at the eastern end of Villers-Bretonneux.

On 4 April, the headquarters of A Company, 35 Battalion was at the western end of the cemetery, 300 metres behind the line, which ran northeast via B Company to the N29. Both companies broke up elements of the 9th BR Division forming up on the D42 but withdrew when the Germans began bypassing them after 41 Brigade bolted. Now isolated because 7/Buffs on its right had already buckled, C Company across the railway pulled back as well. Leaving the cemetery, follow the road around to the N29. Starting 150 metres east of the junction, the Australian support line went 1.4 kilometres south to the old railway bridge at the embankment known as the mound. Vaire and Hamel Woods are to the north.

Turn left onto the N29. The airfields started 400 metres along on the left and continued almost to the roundabout 500 metres further on **(12)**, where 35 Battalion's withdrawal ended. Linking with 1/Royal Dragoons 1,100 metres up the Hamel road, which heads northeast, the Australian line, strengthened by 33 Battalion, ran to the railway bridge at the mound. Towards midday, the 33rd gained the far end of the airfields but the knock-on effect of 55 Brigade's withdrawal during the afternoon resulted in the Australians retiring towards Villers-Bretonneux. With the arrival of 17/Lancers and some armoured cars, they about-turned and recovered the lost ground. 33 and 34 Battalions between them spread to the point just short of the railway bridge reached by Captain Sayers' charge. At 1 am on 5 April, they advanced to the Australian support line, which became the front line.

Holding this sector when the 228th Division attacked on 24 April, 2/Middlesex were trampled by the three tanks of Lieutenant Skopnik's section. The toughest resistance came from the brickworks, which was on the site of the Airplast/Proust complex due south. With the Middlesex gone, 2/Rifle Brigade, holding the line between the N29 and Vaire Wood, was outflanked. The Germans took Villers-Bretonneux and gained a foothold on Hill 104. 15 Brigade's counterattack swung around the northern side of the town and should have gone on to the old front line but mistakenly halted on the Hamel road.

A sign proclaiming *'Villers-Bretonneux l'Australie en Picardie'*, stands on the N29 at the entrance to the town. Topped by a French helmet instead of a British one, the demarcation stone **(13)** opposite marks the limit of the German advance, even though it went through the Bois d'Aquenne to the D523 3.4 kilometres west. Giving a Gallic 'nudge, nudge, wink, wink', the local authorities state that the Germans were in the Bois d'Aquenne for less than 24 hours, that the French fought in the battle on 26 April and that, in any case, they paid for the stone!

On 25 April, B and C Companies, 57 Battalion entered the town between Rue Jules Bonhomme on the right and Rue de Corbie 450 metres further on, opposite which you should turn left onto Rue Maurice Seigneurgens. As you go through the six-way intersection, Rue Driot, where Lieutenant Colonels Goddard and Morshead had their headquarters on 4 April, is on the right. Continue southwards to the railway bridge **(14)**. On 24 April, 2/E. Lancs stretched from the N29 along the eastern side of the road down which you have just come and then swung back at the bridge to parallel the railway. The tanks overran them along with the remnants of 2/W. Yorks, who had formed a hasty defence at the station 150 metres west.

When 57 Battalion and 2/R. Berks were clearing the town, Lieutenant Falconer's men fired from the bridge at the Germans withdrawing on the far side of the railway. 22/DLI took over the clearance in this area so that the two companies of the 57th could link up with the rest of the battalion near the N29 roundabout. The gap with 13 Brigade's left, which rested on the lip of the hollow west of Monument Farm, was not closed until early morning on 26 April. You should now familiarise yourself with the fighting from the roundabout and Crucifix Corner Cemetery vantage points on the D23 **(15)**.

After passing Lancer Wood on the left, your next stop is the track **(16)** that runs due north from the left of the D23 2.6 kilometres from the cemetery. It is on the Aubercourt Spur, from where German machine guns swept the southern end of Hangard Wood East and Hill 99, both of which are across the D23. 20 Battalion's attack on 7 April, in which Captain Storkey won the VC, reached the near side of the wood but suffered heavily from their fire. The Germans counterattacked from the ravine below you and from the Strip Copse re-entrant, which branches off it due west. When they attacked on 12 April, the French artillery smashed 104 RIR as it debouched from Lancer Wood into the ravine.

Now look northeastwards, where the top of the Cross of Sacrifice in Toronto Cemetery is on the skyline. In the attack on 30 March, the 19th Division approached the cemetery location and its skirmishers went through Lancer Wood to the D23. 33

The memorial on the Cachy Road to the tank battle.

Ici, le 24 Avril 1918, eut lieu le premier combat mondial entre tanks allemands et britanniques.

Here, on the 24th of April 1918, the first ever tank battle took place between German and British armor.

Hier, am 24. April 1918, findet der erste Weltangriff zwischen deutschen und britishen Panzerwagen.

167

Battalion and 12/Lancers regained the wood and established a line hugging it that crossed the D23 250 metres north. Holding this sector on 4 April, 6/Northants were driven 1.3 kilometres rearwards by the gas-sodden bombardment before the afternoon attack.

Continue on the D23 for another 650 metres and turn right onto the D76 for Hangard Communal Cemetery Extension (17), 1.1 kilometres along in the shadow of Hill 99. Cemetery and Hangard Copses are respectively right and left on the slope. The British and the Australians between them held the line from Hangard Copse north and the French occupied the cemetery and the village, which changed hands several times before they lost it on 24 April. For Hangard château, take the minor road that heads half left from the crossroads in Hangard.

Return to the D76, turn left and, after 1.8 kilometres, right onto the D934 at Domart. Drive 700 metres through the village and turn right onto the D523. After 1.1 kilometres, you will pass the head of the re-entrant from which 10/Essex counterattacked towards Hangard on 12 April. Then look left to see Gentelles, through which the Gentelles Line ran to the N29. The village was the headquarters of the 18th and 61st Divisions and 9 Brigade, and depth battalions for the front line around Hangard Wood West on the right were deployed near it. Most of the wood was lost on 24 April but 10/Essex and 7/Queen's recaptured the western half during the French counterattack two days later. As you head northwards, imagine the Moroccan Division's assault across the open ground to your right. The gentle slope on the right nearer Cachy was where the Whippets crushed the two battalions of the 77th Reserve Division.

Continue to the road junction on the northern side of Cachy (18). Curving around the opposite end of the village, the Cachy Switch ran to the far corner of the Bois d'Aquenne, which is on the right of the D523 beyond the autoroute bridge. The Bois l'Abbé is on the left. Passing 350 metres from your location, the start line for 13 and 54 Brigades on 24 April went from the bridge southwards. The tanks fought in the fields to the east and Monument Farm is on the skyline almost due east.

After crossing the autoroute, turn right to skirt the southern side of the Bois d'Aquenne. Lieutenant Sadlier won the VC for leading a charge that destroyed many of the German machine guns enfilading 51 Battalion from it. A memorial halfway down the slope commemorates the tank battle. At the bottom of the dip, the road crosses a deep cut and a farm track runs off to the right just beyond a line of bushes (19). A machine gun firing along the wire of the Cachy Switch in this area greatly troubled the Australians. 1/Sherwood Foresters had been shot up earlier as they swung past the near corner of the Bois d'Aquenne to counterattack the town. On 25 April, 2/W. Yorks and three tanks swept north through the wood towards the N29. Some of the Germans retreating across the hollow on the eastern side surrendered when the tanks broke out into it.

The red château, battered but still standing, c1919.

The sunken stretch of road here is the original Cachy road, the rest of which was consumed by the autoroute. Note the remains of roadside dugouts as you continue into the town. 2/Northants' headquarters was under the railway bridge. After the road becomes Rue Victoria, visit

The red château, battlefield visitor attraction, 2003.

the ANZAC Museum in the primary school on the right. Turn left afterwards onto Rue Melbourne, passing the *mairie* on the right just

The red château, makes way for supermarket, 2004. Tower of the Australian National Memorial behind.

before the Place de General de Gaulle. On reaching this point while clearing the town, 57 Battalion and 2/R. Berks had taken 150 prisoners. Turn left onto the N29, where the site of the red château comes up on the right after 300 metres, and continue past the *gendarmerie* to the N29 railway bridge **(20)**. A tank, probably *Cyklop*, lumbered up the tracks to it.

The railway runs past the back of Adelaide Cemetery **(21)**, 300 metres along the N29. Forced out of their original location near the western end of the bridge, the Australian patrols from 59 Battalion joined the survivors of 2/E. Lancs on the far side of the tracks there. After a female tank drove 207 RIR's posts from the area behind the *gendarmerie*, the line moved forward to the Australians' first position. Continue on the N29 for 600 metres and turn right onto the D523, where a POW cage was set up under the railway bridge on 25 April. Lieutenant Butler's 18-pounder was on the embankment 250 metres west of it. The start line for 15 Brigade's counterattack began 500 metres from the bridge and ran along the D523 to a point level with the Australian National Memorial, which can be reached by turning right onto the D23 in Fouilloy.

Walk One. The Attack and Counterattack on 4 April
This eight-kilometre (5 miles) walk starts from Marcelcave Buttes National Cemetery **(1)**. From the western edge of Lamotte-Warfusée, on the N29 2.2 kilometres northeast, the German line ran 900 metres east of your location and passed in front of Marcelcave, 1.3 kilometres southeast across the railway, whose embankment stretches west towards Villers-Bretonneux. The cemetery was the headquarters of A Company, 35 Battalion and lay 300 metres behind its front line. B Company on the left met 8/Rifle Brigade on the N29 and C Company straddled the railway on the right. Remember that the 'line' consisted of widely spaced posts in foxholes and fragments of trench.

Seeing the 9th BR Division assembling before the villages and on the D42 between them, 35 Battalion smashed three attempted attacks and mowed down the 7 am general assault. But 8/Rifle Brigade across the N29 gave way, enabling 14 BRIR to get behind B Company. It had to withdraw, forcing A Company back in conformity. Isolated because 7/Buffs alongside it had already gone, C Company retired as well.

From the cemetery, turn left at the T-junction and follow the road to the N29. As it bends to the right, pick out the old railway bridge a kilometre southwest, which was at the southern end of the Australian support line. C Company gained touch with 7/Buffs there. The

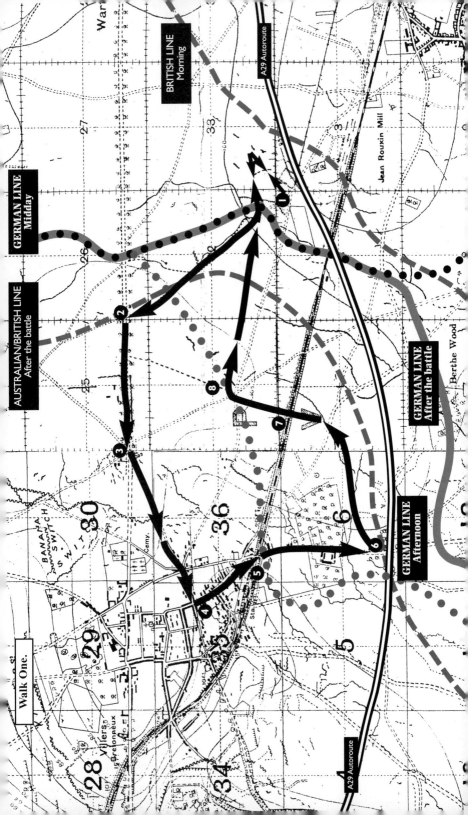

northern end, 1.4 kilometres away, was 150 metres east of the junction with the N29 **(2)**. 41 Brigade, whose collapse sparked the Australian withdrawal, briefly rallied on a line between the N29 and Accroche Wood to the northeast before back-pedalling to 43 Brigade's line on Hill 104, which rises to the northwest.

Sticking to the edge of the field, walk towards Villers-Bretonneux. The airstrips began on the left 400 metres along and continued almost to the roundabout **(3)**, which is where 35 Battalion halted. Moving up from the town, 33 Battalion filled the gaps in the line to the old railway bridge, while its C Company stretched 230 metres along the Hamel Road, which runs northeast towards Vaire Wood. Together with a machine gun section that had set up a post on it half way to the wood, C Company checked 207 RIR's left, which was following up 41 Brigade. At 10.15 am, a squadron of 1/Royal Dragoons connected the Australians to the line on Hill 104. Unable to progress, the Germans retired down the N29, easing the advance of C Company and the cavalry almost to the junction from which you have just come.

When 55 Brigade broke during the afternoon attack, the Australians on the railway swung back to form a defensive flank but those alongside thought they were withdrawing and did the same. B and C Companies from 33 Battalion at the end of the airfields left only when 14 BRIR's advance to the south threatened to cut them off. They u-turned on the arrival of 17/Lancers and took on the Germans as three armoured cars, racing up the N29, also joined in. 14 BRIR stalled and the ground was retaken. 33 and 34 Battalions extended southwards to the position near the old railway bridge reached by the charges of 36 Battalion and Captain Sayers' men.

From the roundabout, head southwest on Rue du Hamel to the town and go over the six-way intersection onto Rue Driot, where Lieutenant Colonels Goddard and Morshead had co-located their headquarters. Cross Rue Melbourne to Rue Victoria and the ANZAC Museum **(4)** is in the primary school on the left. Return to Rue Melbourne, turn right and, at the Place du 14 Juillet, head left along Rue de la Gare to the Place de la Libération, where you swing right onto the D23. In 1918,

The site of the railway bridge at the southern end of the Australian support line.

the town ended at the railway bridge (5) 100 metres ahead. D Company, 35 Battalion under Captain Sayers charged from there along the northern side of the cutting.

After crossing the bridge, consider 36 Battalion's charge and the battle to the south from the roundabout and Crucifix Corner Cemetery vantage points (6), then take the easterly road from the roundabout and pause on the bend after about 600 metres. Monument Wood extended from the D23 to within 200 metres of this location and then ran north for 300 metres. Advancing between the wood and the railway, A Company continued along the railway and B Company swung around the eastern face of the wood. C Company, which attacked on the southern side of Monument Farm, did not get much beyond the roundabout, while 7/Queen's were short of the D23.

Continue to the railway bridge (7) and look east. The next bridge, under which 35 Battalion had set up an aid post, was at the southern end of the Australian support line and can be reached by walking along the edge of the field on the northern side of the cutting. On the other side, the mound was much more prominent then than now. The strongpoint the Germans set up on top at the near end of the bridge stopped Captain Bushelle's charge close to 7/Buffs' old headquarters, which was in the side of the mound 200 metres from the bridge, and Captain Sayers' men on the northern side of the tracks opposite.

Returning to the road, walk 400 metres to the roundabout (8) and take the easterly farm track. It crosses the support line, which was regained early on 5 April, after another 400 metres. Overrunning the mound, D Company, 34 Battalion halted 140 metres beyond the bridge. On this side of the railway, C Company had a tough fight and briefly lost touch with 33 Battalion, which had a sharp encounter itself at the end of the airstrips on the N29. The support line was the front line thereafter.

Walk Two. 24-7 April: North of the Railway
This 9.5 kilometre (6 miles) walk covers the action in and north of Villers-Bretonneux on 24 April, the clearance of the town and the securing of the line around it. After studying the battle from the Australian National Memorial (1), take the northeasterly track from the back of the Memorial, which can be reached via the track that runs along the southern side from the car park, and then the track that heads up Hill 104 to the Hamelet road (2), 15 Brigade's first objective. It was to pivot southeastwards there for the advance on the final objective, the old front line on the far side of the crest that had been occupied by

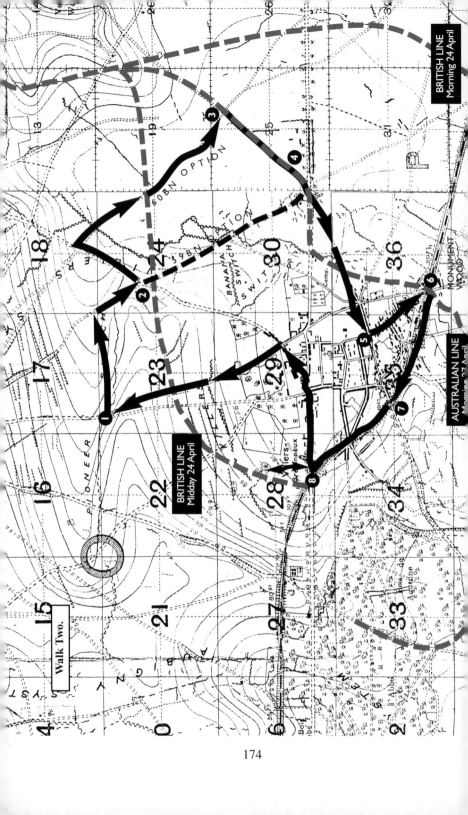

BRITISH LINE
Morning 24 April

AUSTRALIAN LINE

BRITISH LINE
Midday 24 April

Walk Two.

174

2/Rifle Brigade. The Germans at the town end of the road detected the redeployment, prompting the Australian bayonet charge.

Continuing on the track will put you on the left of 59 Battalion and get you to the roundabout on the N29. Heading left on the road for 500 metres and taking the parallel track brings you over the crest on the left of the 60th. The reserve line, or Villers System, crossed the track 200 metres beyond the Hamelet road and the east-west line onto which B Company, 2/Rifle Brigade swivelled went over another 500 metres ahead. Passing through it, 60 Battalion drifted towards the fighting near the town. Unable to gain touch with 54 Battalion, D Company under Lieutenant Simpson formed a defensive flank that started 230 metres further on and ran along the track to the Hamel road **(3)**. As the 54th's right was on the road 600 metres northeast, a large salient existed in the Australian line. Simpson spent 25 April pinned down in it. Pivoting on the Hamel road junction, B and D Companies of the 60th closed the gap early on 27 April. Simpson was among the dead.

Now walk down the Hamel road to the roundabout on the N29 **(4)**, which was on 59 Battalion's right flank. Corporal Rusden's men captured 20 Germans there. The 59th and 60th thought the Hamel road was the final objective and, in so far as the old front line crossed it on the left of 60 Battalion, they were right. Pointing out that it also crossed the N29 1,350 metres ahead, Captain Morgan of the 57th led A and D Companies to that location but they had to return to the roundabout area to avoid being cut off. B and C Companies faced the town on a northwesterly line from the N29 past the end of the first street, Rue Jules Bonhomme, to the Hamelet road.

In the morning, Lieutenant Skopnik's tanks and 207 RIR had overrun 2/Middlesex between the N29 and the railway, which cuts by the gravel works 1.4 kilometres southwest. D Company resisted almost to the end beyond the airfields. 2/Rifle Brigade on the northern side of the N29 was then enveloped and virtually annihilated. Passing your location, I/48 IR and half of III/48 IR occupied the northern part of Villers-Bretonneux, followed later by II/48 IR.

15 Brigade's charge from the Hamelet road.

Villers-Bretonneux railway station today.

Continue southwestwards on the Hamel road. Starting at Rue du 8 Mai, which skirts the industrial zone on your left, the line taken up by the two companies of 57 Battalion after they cleared the town on 25 April crossed 320 metres along and ran to the N29. 2/E. Lancs' line crossed 300 metres further on, a developed area now but mainly open fields in 1918. After 207 RIR broke through, some men fought on in the brickworks, which was in the Airplast site, until Lieutenant Skopnik's tanks surrounded them. *Lotti* and *Alter Fritz* helped mop up the end of the town facing you, although it started further west then.

Going over the six-way intersection, take Rue Driot, which crosses Rue Melbourne to become Rue Victoria. After visiting the ANZAC Museum **(5)** in the primary school on the left, return to Rue Melbourne. By the time the 57 Battalion companies and 2/R. Berks reached the *mairie* a few hundred metres north along it, they had taken 150 prisoners. Heading south, turn left at the fork onto Rue de la Gare for the station, where 2/Northants ended up after dashing across the hollow from 13 Brigade's left on the far side of the tracks. The station was a staging point for Germans withdrawing to Monument Farm. Lieutenant Falconer's platoon caught them there and at the bridge over the D23, 150 metres east, until it was withdrawn to a position on Rue du 8 Mai near the intersection.

Now walk to the bridge **(6)**. 22/DLI met stubborn resistance in this area. Two companies of 49 Battalion moved through it to link up with the right flank of the 57th at 1 am on 26 April, establishing a continuous line between 13 and 15 Brigades. Before leaving, look

176

along the railway in both directions. Chased by Lieutenant Skopnik's tank, which trundled to the far end of the town, Captain Brodie's men escaped down the tracks, as did 2/W. Yorks after briefly rallying south of the station.

Villers-Bretonneux more or less stopped at the railway in 1918. You can follow it by crossing the bridge and heading right on the Chemin Latéral, which progressively becomes Boulevard Jean-Jaurès/Victor Collet/St Martin before meeting the N29 after 1.8 kilometres. Swinging around the bridge, 2/E. Lancs' line paralleled the left of the Chemin Latéral. German machine guns fired into the Australian flank from the embankment, which formed a rampart around the southwestern side of the town. 2/Northants' headquarters on 25 April was under the bridge on the Cachy road **(7)**. On 24 April, 93 RIR had raced across the next bridge to the Bois d'Aquenne, covered by Lieutenant Uihlein's tanks. One of them, probably *Cyklop*, rattled up the tracks to the bridge on the N29 **(8)**.

Cross the N29 and walk up Rue du Sémaphore, which starts on the right of the bridge. Seeing the tank, and 93 RIR breaking out of the town, 59 Battalion's patrols withdrew from their position 100 metres along and joined the survivors of 2/E. Lancs 140 metres further back. This line reoccupied the Australians' original position after a British female tank overran 207 IR's advanced posts on the slope behind the *gendarmerie* to the east.

Heading back into the town on the N29, you will pass the site of the red château before turning left onto Rue Mme Delacourt-Rousseau after 750 metres. The Hamelet Road, astride which 57 Battalion's two companies and 2/R. Berks entered Villers-Bretonneux, is directly ahead on the crossroads 300 metres along. You should turn left there onto Rue de Corbie, the D23, for the Australian National Memorial 1.6 kilometres further on.

Walk Three. 24-27 April: South of the Railway
Starting from the crossroads at the northern edge of Cachy **(1)**, this 10.5 kilometre (6.5 miles) walk traces the fighting between the railway and Hangard Wood. After passing in front of the village, the Cachy Switch swung northeast 320 metres from your location. Straddling the autoroute, the D523 separates the Bois l'Abbé on the left from the Bois d'Aquenne, which 1/Sherwood Foresters were thought to be holding, on the right. The Germans actually held it, forcing 13 Brigade's start line, which began at the wood and should have passed 500 metres ahead of you, to be laid 270 metres closer. The objective was 1.3

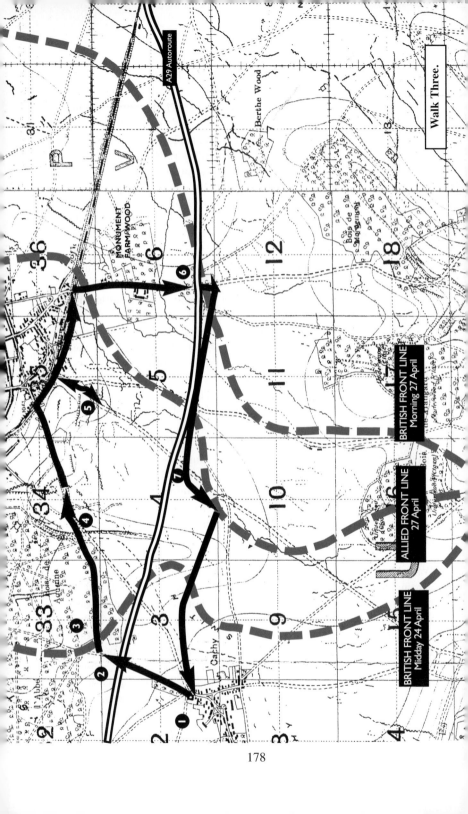

A29 Autoroute

Berthe Wood

Walk Three.

MONUMENT
FARM WOOD

Bois de
Morgemont

Cachy

BRITISH FRONT LINE
Morning 27 April

ALLIED FRONT LINE
27 April

BRITISH FRONT LINE
Midday 24 April

kilometres beyond Monument Farm, which is in the copse surmounted by twin poplars on the skyline immediately to the left of the autoroute. 54 Brigade and the Moroccan Division attacked to the southeast, where you can see Lancer Wood behind Hangard Wood. *Nixe* fought Lieutenant Mitchell's tank in the fields to the east.

Cross the autoroute bridge (2), which offers an elevated vantage point from which to consider these events, and head right past the Bois d'Aquenne. The old Cachy road, which tracked well to the south here, fell victim to the autoroute but the new stretch puts you almost on the scene of Lieutenant Sadlier's VC action on 24 April (3). Look south to see how I/5 Guard Grenadier and the nine guns of the regimental machine gun company, strung out along the edge of the wood, enfiladed 51 Battalion as it advanced across the slope.

A memorial to the tank duel is halfway down the hill on the left. At the bottom of the dip, the original Cachy road passes over a deep cut marked by a line of scrubby bushes on the right (4). Caught there around 12.30 pm on 24 April as they swung north towards Villers-Bretonneux after moving along the southern side of the wood, 1/Sherwood Foresters were flung back to the D523. A machine gun sited in the vicinity of the farm track beyond the cut to fire along the wire of the Cachy Switch, which paralleled the road 180 metres south, inflicted dreadful casualties on the Australians trying to get through it in their counterattack that evening.

After a hundred or so metres, climb the northern bank of the now sunken road. Covered by *Baden 1*, *Cyklops*, *Herkules* and Tank 541, 93 RIR and 5 Guard Grenadiers moved through Villers-Bretonneux and along the hollow between your location and the town into the Bois d'Aquenne. They withdrew early on 25 April after 2/W. Yorks and Captain Houlton's three tanks entered the wood from the south. Some of those caught when the tanks emerged on the side facing you surrendered. During the night, 2/Northants had shaken out on the right of the road 350 metres along for the southerly assault on the town but were mauled by the machine guns on the railway as they descended the slope. Keep an eye out for the remains of roadside dugouts as you walk to the spot.

Turn right onto the Chemin des Carrières a couple of hundred metres short of the bridge and right again at the end of it onto Rue du Gazomètre. At the fork, take the right branch for 170 metres (5). You are now on 13 Brigade's left flank on the old Domart road, which A Company, 51 Battalion occupied after withdrawing from the D23 north of Monument Farm. Stretching westwards in a defensive flank above

179

13 Brigade's advance on 24 April 1918.

Dugout remains on the Cachy Road.

How the machine gun on the Cachy Switch wire caught 13 Brigade.

the hollow, 2/Northants fired on the Germans escaping from the Bois d'Aquenne. Subsequently catching III/5 Foot Guards at Monument Farm unawares, the Northants dashed across to the station area. Probing eastwards from your location to the D23 bridge on the night of 25 April, patrols from 50 Battalion met patrols from 49 Battalion that had linked up with 15 Brigade.

Returning to Rue du Gazomètre, walk north along it to the Chemin Latéral and turn right for the D23, where you turn right again. A Company, 51 Battalion reached the D23 this side of Monument Farm, which is ahead of you on the right. Go past it and consider the fighting from the roundabout and Crucifix Corner Cemetery vantage points **(6)**, before heading west from the old D23 crossroads at the cemetery's southeastern corner. 7/Bedfords thought they had gained the old British front line, which crossed 450 metres along, but were really on the support line 270 metres further west. Shelled there, they withdrew beyond the Hangard road, 180 metres rearwards, on which *Elfriede* had ditched just across the autoroute. Their retirement forced the Australians back.

The new line ran behind the Domart road, which you reach at a T-junction **(7)**. 13 Brigade caught parts of II/5 Foot Guards at field kitchens on it to the north. Machine guns dotting the area between the road and the Cachy Switch decimated 7/RW Kents, who were attacking to the southwest. One in the field to the south prevented the survivors gaining touch with the Bedfords. The Germans penetrated the gap on 25 April but the Bedfords' bayonet charge ejected them. Throughout the day, 54 Brigade's line was thought to be east of the Domart road, even though the Bedfords were 180 metres west of it. The Whippets' foray towards Hangard Wood confirmed that the Germans were also west of the road. The reports were disbelieved.

Consequently, the Moroccan Division, which planned to attack from the Domart road, came under fire well before reaching it. Stretching north and south in broad daylight, the assault barely got beyond your location. Forming up on the right of Hangard Wood West, 10/Essex and 7/Queen's recaptured half of the wood in the day's only success. Walk south on the Domart road and then head for Cachy, which you can see ahead. Captain Price's Whippets crossed the road 600 metres along to rampage through two battalions of the 77th Reserve Division in the fields to the south. 2/10 Londons had been shot down in them earlier while trying to restore the line north of Hangard Wood. The crossroads from whence you started is another kilometre west.

Walk Four. The Hangard Flank

This 5.4 kilometre (3.4 miles) walk starts from Hangard Communal Cemetery Extension (1), which is in the shadow of Hill 99. As you look north, Hangard and Cemetery Copses are respectively left and right. Ejected from the cemetery and its copse on 4 April, the French 141 Regiment withdrew to the western end of Hangard and connected with 6/Northants, whose original line had run almost to the D23, at Hangard Copse. The French retook the cemetery during a joint counterattack with the Northants on 5 April, briefly lost it on 9 April, lost it again, together with Hangard Copse and Hangard on 12 April and promptly regained all but the cemetery in a joint counterattack with 10/Essex. On 15 April, the French took the cemetery but A Company, 18 Battalion failed to hold onto Cemetery Copse. The French were driven beyond Hangard on 24 April.

If you want to see Hangard château, take the minor road that heads half left from the village crossroads. Otherwise, turn right onto the Cachy road, which swings north 350 metres past the chicken battery on the left and reaches the crest of Hill 99 at a trigonometric marker 400 metres further on (2). The two parts of Hangard Wood are north of you and the line of bushes 400 metres northeast marks the Strip Copse re-entrant. Lancer Wood is on the far side of the D23. After the attack on 4 April, the British line ran from Hangard Copse to your location and then along the road before bending around the front of Hangard Wood West on the Villers-Bretonneux road. It had been on the far side of Lancer Wood. When 107 RIR captured Hangard Copse and the village on 12 April, 10/Essex regained the copse after advancing over a kilometre, mostly under shellfire, across the fields to the west.

Continue to the corner of Hangard Wood West (3). On 24 April, 3/Londons held the line to the south but 2/2 Londons abandoned all except this bit of the wood and withdrew west of the Cachy Road when 2/4 Londons crumpled on their left. 10/Essex and 7/Queen's formed up near the road two days later and recaptured the wood up to the main north-south ride, which you can reach by walking 150 metres along the

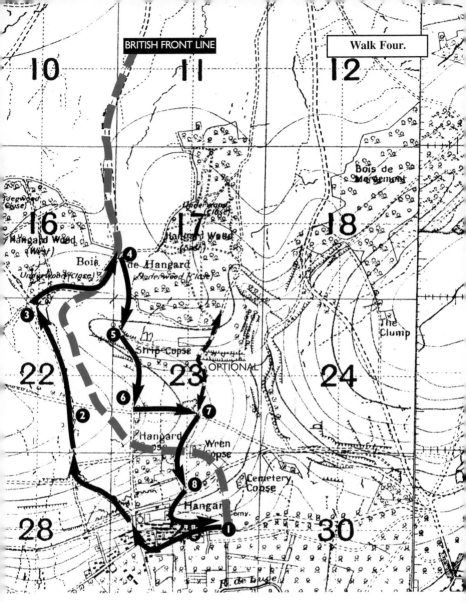

southern edge. Passing Hangard Wood British Cemetery after 300 metres, continue to the far corner, where the two woods touch **(4)**, and look north. 7/RW Kents reformed on the Villers-Bretonneux road between them after being driven back from Lancer Wood on 4 April. 8/R. Berks retired to the road beyond the northern end of Hangard Wood East after almost being wiped out in a counterattack.

Entering that end of wood in the Australian attack on 7 April, Lieutenant Storkey's men routed the Germans who were lacerating B

183

The Hangard battlefield from the location of the strongpoint overrun by Lieutenant Thompson's platoon on 15 April 1918.

Company, 19 Battalion as it assaulted from Hangard Wood West 400 hundred metres north of your location. B Company then pushed through to the far side of Hangard Wood East, access to which was prohibited at the time of writing, but withdrew on finding it untenable. Storkey won the VC. Now head south on the Villers-Bretonneux road, which is just a track as it skirts the near side. C Company, 20 Battalion's assault, which was easier, plunged into the wood in this area.

After 700 metres, you will cross the Strip Copse re-entrant **(5)** and start up Hill 99. During 18 Battalion's attack on Cemetery Copse on 15 April, B Company set up two posts 200 metres apart in the field on your right. Lieutenant Thompson's platoon was to have set up another 100 metres south of the re-entrant in the field on your left but overran instead a German strongpoint that Thompson discovered at the crossroads 150 metres further south **(6)**. Trying to capture a known strongpoint 450 metres east on the next crossroads **(7)**, to which you should now walk, Lieutenant McLaren's platoon was smashed 20 metres short. The Aubercourt Spur is the high ground across the ravine and Toronto Cemetery is visible to the right of Marcelcave church on the horizon.

In C Company, 20 Battalion's attack on Hangard Wood East on 7 April, German machine guns on the Aubercourt Spur turned the eastern edge of the wood into a death trap and helped counterattacks from the ravine and the Strip Copse re-entrant. They also swept away the platoon tasked to give C Company flank protection from your current location at the eastern crossroads, whereupon the Germans emplaced machine guns here to flay the southern end of the wood and cover infiltration along the re-entrant behind C Company. It clung to

Strip Copse   Lancer Wood   Aubercourt Spur

the wood's southwestern corner but eventually had to withdraw. B Company, 19 Battalion was long gone, forced from the northern end of the wood by the Germans on the distant knuckle of high ground between it and Lancer Wood.

As an optional extra that will give you a better view, take the northerly track, which goes over the Strip Copse re-entrant and up the eastern side of Hangard Wood East. As you walk, note the remains of shell holes on your right. How far you go is your decision but you

'Shell hole remains as seen from the track north of the Strip Copse re-entrant.'

should at least approach the wood, which will also bring you closer to the knuckle that ended B Company's battle. Returning to the crossroads, look back at Lancer Wood, from which 104 RIR streamed towards Hangard on 12 April. The French artillery plastered the Germans as they tried to cross the ravine below you, which helped give it the nickname 'Death Valley'.

Now continue southwards for 450 metres to the cross track **(8)** between Hangard and Cemetery Copses. Approaching along the sunken road from the west in the attack on 15 April, A Company, 18 Battalion formed up in the fields 180 metres this side of Cemetery Copse, charged and took it but was pinned down by heavy fire. Carrying parties trying to get through were stopped short of the northern edge. The copse fell silent but the French, attacking alongside, took the cemetery below you.

SELECT BIBLIOGRAPHY

I relied heavily in the writing of this guide on instructions, orders and reports relating to the Villers-Bretonneux/Hangard battles, and the war diaries of the divisions, brigades and battalions that participated, all of which the Australian War Memorial in Canberra and The National Archives in London hold between them. The files I found most useful, as well as personal manuscripts, are listed in the notes at the end of each chapter.

The following secondary sources describe the fighting or specific aspects of it:

C. Barnett, 'Offensive 1918' in N. Frankland & C. Dowling (eds.), *Decisive Battles of the Twentieth Century* (Hutchinson, 1976).

C. Barnett, *The Swordbearers*, (Papermac, 1986).

C.E.W. Bean, *Anzac to Amiens* (AWM, 1968).

C.E.W. Bean, *The Official History of Australia in the War of 1914-1918. V. The AIF in France During The Main German Offensive*, 1918 (Angus & Robertson, 1941).

G. Blaxland, *Amiens 1918* (Star, 1981).

J.H. Boraston and C.E.O. Bax, *The Eighth Division* 1914-1918 (Medici Society, 1926).

M. Brown, *The Imperial War Museum Book of 1918* (Sidgwick & Jackson, 1998).

N. Browning, *Fix Bayonets* (Browning, 2000).

P.J. Campbell, *The Ebb and Flow of Battle* (OUP, 1979).

D. Coombes, *Morshead* (OUP, 2001).

F.M. Cutlack, *The Australians: Their Final Campaign, 1918* (Sampson, Low & Marston, 1919).

W.H. Downing, *To The Last Ridge* (Duffy & Snellgrove, 1998).

J.E. Edmonds, *Military Operations: France and Belgium, 1918. I. The German March Offensive* (Macmillan, 1935).

J.E. Edmonds, *Military Operations: France and Belgium, 1918. II. March-April: Continuation of the German Offensives* (Macmillan, 1937).

J. Edwards, *Never A Backward Step. A History of the First 33rd Battalion AIF* (Bettong Books, 1996).

A.D. Ellis, *The Story of the Fifth Australian Division* (Hodder and Stoughton, 1920).

H. Essame, *The Battle for Europe 1918* (Scribners, 1972).

D. Fletcher (ed.), *Tanks and Trenches* (Alan Sutton, 1994).

H. Gough, *The Fifth Army* (Hodder & Stoughton, 1931).

A. Home, *The Diary of a World War 1 Cavalry Officer* (Costello, 1985).

B.H. Liddell Hart, *The Tanks,* (Cassell, 1959).

P.H. Liddle, *The Soldiers' War, 1914-1918* (Blandford, 1988).

N. Lytton, *The Press and the General Staff* (Collins, 1920).

L. Macdonald, *To The Last Man* (Viking, 1998).

K.W. Mackenzie, *The Story of the Seventeenth Battalion AIF in The Great War* (privately published, 1946).

F.B. Maurice, *The Life of General Lord Rawlinson of Trent* (Cassell, 1928).

R. McMullin, *Pompey Elliott* (Scribe, 2002).

M. Middlebrook, *The Kaiser's Battle* (Allen Lane, 1978).

G.H.F. Nichols, *The 18th Division in the Great War* (William Blackwood, 1922).

B. Pitt, *1918 The Last Act* (Papermac, 1984).

P. Simkins, 'For Better or Worse: Sir Henry Rawlinson and his Allies in 1916 and 1918' in M. Hughes and M. Seligmann (eds.), *Leadership in Conflict* (Leo Cooper, 2000).

P. Simkins, 'The War Experience of a Typical Kitchener Division: The 18th Division, 1914-18' in H. Cecil and P. Liddle (eds.), *Facing Armageddon* (Leo Cooper, 1996).

P. Slowe and R. Woods, *Fields of Death*, (Robert Hale, 1986).

Selective Index